How to Be Single

The Art & Science of Being Happy and Comfortable Alone

By: Discover Press

ALL RIGHTS RESERVED

No part of this book may be reproduced, stored in a retrieval system, or transmitted in any form or by any means, electronic, mechanical, photocopying, recording, scanning, or otherwise, without the prior written permission of the publisher.

Limit of Liability/Disclaimer of Warranty: the publisher and the author make no representations or warranties with respect to the accuracy or completeness of the contents of this work and specifically disclaim all warranties, including without limitation warranties of fitness for a particular purpose. No warranty may be created or extended by sales or promotional materials. The advice and strategies contained herein may not be suitable for every situation. This work is sold with the understanding that the publisher is not engaged in rendering medical, legal or other professional advice or services. If professional assistance is required, the services of a competent professional person should be sought. Neither the publisher nor the author shall be liable for damages arising herefrom. The fact that an individual, organization or website is referred to in this work as a citation and/or potential source of further information does not mean that the author or the publisher endorses the information the individuals, organization or website may provide or recommendations they/it may make. Further, readers should be aware that websites listed on this work may have changed or disappeared between when this work was written and when it is read.

Table of Contents

INTRODUCTION 6

PART I: SINGLE VS. SOCIETY 8

CHAPTER 1: GIVING UP THE SEARCH: HOW TO KNOW WHEN TO STOP LOOKING FOR A RELATIONSHIP 9

CHAPTER 2: WHY ARE YOU SINGLE? ANSWERING THE QUESTION FOR YOURSELF 14

CHAPTER 3: WHY ARE YOU SINGLE? ANSWERING THE QUESTION FOR OTHERS 19

CHAPTER 4: IT'S NOT YOU AND IT'S NOT THEM 24

CHAPTER 5: INVESTING TIME ELSEWHERE: FAMILY AND FRIENDSHIPS ARE IMPORTANT TOO 29

PART II: HOW TO BE SINGLE: BEING TRULY HAPPY AND COMFORTABLE WHEN YOU'RE SINGLE 33

CHAPTER 6: IT'S ABOUT MORE THAN JUST PHYSICAL ENERGY 35

   BURNOUT *35*

   EMOTIONAL ENERGY *36*

   MENTAL ENERGY *37*

   IDENTIFYING ENERGY DRAINS *38*

   HOW TO REGAIN YOUR ENERGY *39*

CHAPTER 7: CHANGING YOUR BRAIN 41

   CHALLENGE: *42*

   A QUICK NOTE ON HOW TO ADJUST TO BEING SINGLE *45*

CHAPTER 8: GROW AS YOU GO 49

CHAPTER 9: COMFORT IN ALONE TIME 53

CHAPTER 10: "ALONE" DOESN'T HAVE TO MEAN "LONELY" 57

CHAPTER 11: JOY IN THE LITTLE THINGS 62

CHAPTER 12: UNDERSTANDING YOUR COMFORT LEVEL 67

PART III: HOW TO BE SINGLE: DO WHAT YOU LOVE AND LOVE WHAT YOU DO 74

CHAPTER 13: ME TIME 76

CHAPTER 14: WELCOME, WEEKEND! 83

  OUT ON THE TOWN 83

  TABLE FOR ONE 84

  THE STAYCATION 86

  THE DAY TRIP 87

  NOTHING LIKE A JOB WELL DONE 89

  FRIENDLY COMPETITION 90

CHAPTER 15: HAVE TIME, WILL TRAVEL 92

CHAPTER 16: SOCIAL NIGHT 97

PART IV: WHERE DOES YOUR JOURNEY END? 104

CHAPTER 17: LIFESTYLE OR CIRCUMSTANCE? HOW TO FIGURE OUT IF YOU WANT TO BE SINGLE LONG TERM 106

CHAPTER 18: CHAPTER 3 BUT IMAGINED DIFFERENTLY 114

CHAPTER 19: BEING INDEFINITELY SINGLE: WHAT THEY DON'T TELL YOU 124

PART V: AT THE END OF THE ROAD 131

EXTRAS 135

Hobby and Activity Ideas for the Active Person (That You Can Do Without Making It Weird) 136

Hobby and Activity Ideas for the Sedentary Person (That Won't Make You Feel Lonely) 138

Resources for Classes and Learning about Activities in Your City 140

Staycation Ideas and Inspiration Sources 142

Safety Tips for Traveling Alone 147

Budget Friendly Travel Tips and Tricks 150

Ready for Anything Road Trip Packing List 153

Journaling Prompts for at Home 156

Journaling Prompts for Travel 159

Introduction

So, you're single. Maybe you always have been, maybe being single is new for you. The good news is, you're not alone! There are countless people trying to navigate being single and all the feelings and experiences that go along with it. Yet no matter how many single people there are in the world, society still has this idea that you need a significant other in your life in order to be truly happy.

If you're tired of that message but not sure how to fully enjoy your life as a single person, keep reading! This book will dive into everything from weekend plans to tackling the question of why you're single and how to answer it. There's no perfect checklist for how to magically become comfortable and happy alone, but we're going to get pretty close. Hopefully by the time you're done reading, you'll feel much more settled in your singleness and have a whole new way of looking at yourself and your time as a single person. Be patient and kind to yourself, and in case you're feeling down already, spoiler alert: you can actually be happy and comfortable as a single person! Keep reading to find out how!

There's no reason to exclude yourself from happiness when you're not in a relationship. The advice in these chapters will get you as far as you let it, and if you take it to heart (and maybe come back to it a few times), you'll find out there's a whole new world out there for singles that you'll honestly enjoy. You'll get the answers to questions about your relationship status down pat, set up fun things to do by yourself, and make a bucket list of wild things to do while you're single that'll have you genuinely excited for the weekends! So, get comfortable, grab some water, and get ready for some serious singles advice.

Part I: Single vs. Society

This may not seem like a big deal, but what society tells you and how you interact with a relationship-centered society really does affect your comfort level and happiness with being single.

You'll see a recurring theme throughout this book of emphasizing how your mindset and mental health have a massive impact on your comfort and happiness as a single person. In this section, we're going to get into how you view your own singleness, how to respond when other people bring it up, and how to cope with the media message that you can only be happy in a relationship. Keep in mind that changing your mentality is a process and isn't the same for everyone, but the steps are fairly similar for everyone. Once you nail down being confident in your singleness in your own mind, everything will come to you much more easily. Trust the process and you'll be thankful you did!

Chapter 1: Giving Up the Search: How to Know When to Stop Looking for a Relationship

Odds are, if you're reading this, you're already single. If you're still on the fence about continuing your search for a romantic relationship, it's good to see that you're doing your homework! It's understandable if you feel conflicted about whether to give up the search for your perfect partner. Whether you've been burned by the process before or you've never found the right person, it's a big decision to call off the search.

So, how do you know when to stop looking for a relationship? There's really no one-size-fits-all answer to that question. To find out for yourself what's right for you, take a look at your schedule for a week and see how much time you're devoting to searching for a partner. Then compare it to everything else you've got to take care of every day. Are you falling behind on things? Are there tasks you wish you could accomplish that have to fall by the wayside because you're spending all your free time looking for a partner? That could be a sign that you should call off the search for a little while.

Of course, that shouldn't be the only factor upon which you base your decision, but it's a red flag if you've been neglecting things you want to or have to do in favor of looking for a partner. Moderation in how you spend your time is key in maintaining happiness and your ability to handle stresses like looking for a partner. If how you use your time is out of balance, it's probably worth taking a break from looking for a relationship to work on yourself so you find the search less taxing when you decide to pick it back up again.

Another red flag that's probably telling you to stop looking for a relationship is your success rate. If you're having a hard time finding someone or you keep having bad experiences dating, it's probably time to take a break for a little while. Now, your dating success rate is affected by a lot of circumstances that are not under your control, but there are some key factors that you actually *can* control. Things like where you're meeting potential partners, the dating pool, and what you're looking for in a partner and relationship can all contribute to an excellent or terrible success rate when it comes to dating.

The following paragraph is in no way meant to place blame – keep that in mind as you read on. But it's helpful to know what might be causing the search for a relationship to be more trouble than it's worth. We all strike out sometimes—that's totally okay and no reason to feel bad about yourself.

You've probably heard the phrase "looking for love in all the wrong places" before. As cliché as it is, where you go to find potential partners really does have an effect on how successful you'll be in finding your perfect match. So before you decide to call it quits, have you tried looking in other social pools for a romantic match? Maybe dating apps in your city don't offer what you're looking for. Maybe the bar scene just isn't it in your neighborhood. Try mixing it up and see if a new social pool helps you find someone before you call off your search entirely.

If you feel like you're doing everything right and your search is still not turning up any matches, that's okay. It's discouraging, but certainly not uncommon or something to be ashamed of. One of the worst things you can do for yourself long term is settle for someone just because you don't want to be alone. Keep your standards and wait until the right person comes along. Sometimes that right person will cross your path when you least expect it. Have faith in that and try taking a break from actively looking for a partner. Instead, see if someone comes along in your daily life.

Now that you've dedicated some time to exploring why you might not have found someone even though you're investing a lot of time and effort into looking, let's talk about how you might be feeling about your search and about the prospect of choosing to stop the search for now.

For some people, it's easy to make the decision. In fact, your mind may have already been made up before you even started reading. Having your mind made up doesn't negate some nerves, though, because society has spent so long telling us that we need a romantic relationship in order to be happy. It also heavily implies that there's something wrong with us when we're single. It's okay to wonder "what if the right person comes along the day after I delete the dating app?" Or, "what if I never find someone?"

But here's the thing: if that person was "right" for you, they would have been put in your path while you were still on the dating site. The right person will always be in front of you at the right time in both of your lives. We'll talk more about that in a later chapter, but it's worth mentioning now. As far as not finding someone, "never" is a strong word. Just because you've stopped looking for now, doesn't mean that you won't start looking again somewhere down the line or that you won't meet someone organically as you're going about your daily life. Trust your gut: if you feel as though you should stop looking for a relationship, don't let your culture make you feel nervous or guilty for the choice that's right for you.

If you're feeling much less settled in your decision to try out the single lifestyle, then you've come to the right place. The following chapters will cover everything from figuring out how to explain why you're single to other people to how to make the most of your time as a single person. It's much easier to go toward something than run away from something else, so hopefully the insights in Part III of this book will inspire you to make the most of being single and find what makes you the happiest and most comfortable as a single person.

If you're feeling hopeless and depressed because you're not finding a match, and like there must be something wrong with you because you haven't found someone, that's a normal feeling. But you're probably thinking that way because of outside influences, too. It's not fair to you that you're beating yourself up over something that's not all the way within your control. You might be feeling depressed because most cultures tell their young people that you'll be happier when you have someone, or even that you need a romantic relationship to feel happy and validated as a person. While the media often paints these statements in a good light, it's important to remember that you are capable of making your own happiness without a romantic relationship. You could also be burnt out on looking for a relationship. It takes a lot of time and energy to keep putting yourself out there and dealing with all the complications that go along with trying to find a romantic partner. Maybe it's time to take a break, re-center yourself, and recover from that burnout so you can come at dating with fresh energy later.

So, you've made the choice to be single and put down the dating app. What now? How do you tell people (if you have to) that you're not looking for anyone right now? How do you justify it in your own mind? The next two chapters are your first steps to ensuring your comfort as a single person.

Before we move on, it's worth highlighting that being single is a choice, and you have to own it for any of this advice to work for you. Owning the choice to be single doesn't mean you have to brag about it, or that you have to force yourself to be confident in it automatically. Owning your decision is all about understanding that you do have control over your relationships, whether you stay in the dating game, and when, if ever, you get back into it.

As you progress through this book, you'll build confidence in your decision and that confidence will directly translate to how comfortable you are as a single person. It all starts with answering a key question for yourself.

Chapter 2: Why Are You Single? Answering the Question for Yourself

The question of why you're single has likely haunted you at some point in your life if it isn't haunting you now. It's totally normal to be a little bothered by this, and the best thing you can do for yourself is to investigate that feeling. Even if you decided to give up the search voluntarily (no breakups involved), this is still a very important question to answer for both yourself and others. The thing is, there's no one-size-fits-all answer for why you're single. Everyone has reasons that are unique to them. The first step to figuring out how to enjoy being single is finding the answer to the question of *why* you're single—in a way that you can accept and truly stand behind. Being single is, to some extent, a choice, and it is certainly a mentality that you can own and love just like anything else.

Start by asking yourself that question out loud. Go ahead. No one's going to judge you. Now answer yourself without thinking first. What did you say? That first-ditch answer will tell you a lot about what you're really thinking about your relationship status. Don't judge yourself for whatever you said. We're going to work on it. Even if you said, "I don't know," that's okay. Let's go through some possible answers and what you can do with them.

If your answer was something about how you feel pressured to be with someone because you don't want to be alone forever, or you don't want to be judged by everyone else for not having a significant other, don't worry. Lots of people feel that way. That way of thinking is also a big reason why so many people are unhappy when they're single. So, here's big secret number one: Just because you're single now doesn't mean you're going to be single forever.

What if you genuinely want to be in a relationship and it's just not working right now? Be patient. One of the worst things you can do for yourself and your mental health is try to force a relationship when it's just not the right time. While you're in this phase of being single, take some time to learn more about yourself. If you're having trouble finding the right partner, sometimes it helps to spend some time with yourself first. Once you know what you like and have had the chance to follow your own preferences, it's a lot easier to welcome someone new into your life.

If you honestly don't want a relationship at the moment, and you're just feeling pressure from society and the media to be with someone, that's okay. The best advice is to find a way to accept that and become secure in your decision. Hopefully this helps: You're valid for not wanting a relationship. Take a moment and let that sink in. It might help to add that to any affirmations you do during your routine. (If you just read that last sentence and are wondering what in the world affirmations are, they'll be explained in a later chapter—don't worry!)

Affirmations aside, not wanting to be in a relationship is your personal choice, and whether society understands it or not, you can come to a place where you don't feel as though you have to apologize to yourself or other people for it. Whether it's because you had a bad relationship experience, you're so busy you can't imagine trying to make time to meet someone, or you just want to figure out your own life first, be honest with yourself. Own the decision, and whenever you start feeling bad about being single, just remind yourself of the reason you're thinking of now. Eventually, you'll stop feeling guilty at all!

If you've had a bad experience dating, things might be a little more complicated for you. That's a hard thing to go through, and there's probably some healing that needs to happen before you're in a place where you're ready to answer the question "why are you single?" in any way other than with what happened in your last relationship. Time heals most wounds, and sometimes talking with someone helps. Even if you feel like you should be over it by now, if you're still struggling with explaining your singleness to yourself, odds are it's because of your past relationship and you're just not ready to admit that. Since you're here, it seems like now is the time. It's okay. There are so many resources out there to help you heal from your past relationship and get you ready to honestly answer the question: do you still want to be in a relationship someday or do you just feel like you have to? You'll get there. Don't worry. There are books, podcasts, and professionals available to help you process your experiences, so take advantage of them!

All of this is well and good, but most of us have been taught by society and the media for years that you need to be in a relationship to be happy. How do we unlearn that? Once we do, it is so much easier to be happy with your answer of why you're single, especially if it's just "I don't want to be in a relationship right now," and to believe in the possibility of happiness as a single person.

Since the media is such a big part of our daily lives, try to find a TV show, a book, or a movie that promotes a positive message about being single (those are hard to find, but they are out there—so-called "chick flicks" sometimes have that message), and try to find a fictitious icon for how you want your time as a single person to play out. Try to find other media like that one and slowly replace the shows that made you wish you had a partner with ones that give you a new idea for how to spend your weekend. Unlearning a cultural view is not an easy task, but since you're reading this, you're already on your way!

As you're discovering the answer to why you're single, start redefining how you view it. Instead of answering in the negative, such as, "I don't have the energy," try reframing it: "I want to spend my limited energy on my own growth." This kind of positive verbiage really helps you see being single as a good thing much faster.

Before we move on to how to answer the "why are you single?" question when other people ask you, please remind yourself that the answer you give yourself is allowed to change. It likely will at some point in your life. That doesn't make what you answer now and your reason behind it less valid, it just means you've changed as a person—which is, after all, the mark of a mature person.

If you remember nothing else from this part of the book, please remember to be kind and patient with yourself as you go through this process of learning to enjoy your singleness.

Chapter 3: Why Are You Single? Answering the Question for Others

So, now you've figured out the answer to your singleness for your own peace of mind. But what do you say to other people when they comment on your relationship status?

These days, those questions take a lot of different shapes and come at you in a lot of ways you may not expect, but don't be alarmed! Once you know the real reason why you choose to be single, it's much easier to explain to other people. Before we begin, there's a recurring theme that will run through this chapter and it's an important thing to keep in mind as you're reading: Don't be defensive. Being casual and open about being single goes a long way in stopping probing questions or lines of discussion that you'd rather not participate in, and it comes from a place of self-assurance and comfort in the answers you found in the last chapter. Now, let's take a look at how other people respond to you being single and how to tackle the assumptions and comments you'll likely get at some point in your life if you haven't already.

First off, assumptions. The assumption that you need to be in a relationship in order to be happy is what typically drives people to ask those kinds of questions. Ordinarily, those questions are coming from a good place (or at the very least a place of blissful unawareness); it helps to keep that in mind so you're not defensive when the subject comes up. Knowing that you don't have to agree with those assumptions also helps you hold firm to your decision to be happy as a single person.

How do you deal with those assumptions in the media and in person? The reality is, if we tried to cut all relationship-centric media out of our lives, we wouldn't have much media left to consume. And that's not the answer, anyway! Relationships make for excellent comedic relief and help lots of plot points, but the trick is to find media that doesn't send the message that you'll only be happy when you're in a relationship. Only you know what kind of media is good for your mental health, so just keep this in mind when you're looking for a movie to watch on a Saturday night. If you're already feeling a little down, maybe don't turn on that rom-com and find a good old-fashioned comedy instead.

When people assume in conversations that you're looking for a relationship, or you are feeling sad because you don't have anyone at the moment, you have a few response choices depending on the person you're speaking with and the context of the conversation. You can either not correct them and just play along, which might be the easiest thing if you don't really want to explain your reasons for being single, or you can explain why you enjoy being single.

Most times, it's just easier not to correct people and trust your inner strength to get you through the rest of that conversation. Vague comments and avoiding the use of the word "we" helps keep people off your back. The key thing about this type of approach, however, is that how you're feeling will show on your face. So if you're truly still down on yourself for being single, it'll show. If you've already found your happiness in being single, your confidence and comfort will show through and it'll be like you're having any other conversation.

If you feel that it's the right time and place to explain that you're single and like it that way, or you have to so that you're not misleading someone, then it begs the question of how to respond. When people are making comments like "you should get out more," and "you'll find someone," or they are giving you unsolicited advice, it's easy to respond defensively. We all do it, even if we're the happiest we've ever been as single people! Sometimes it's just annoying to have to explain it one more time. One of the best responses that's easy to keep on the tip of your tongue is "Maybe someday. I'm happy right now, though."

It's such a strange thing that people feel as though their choice to be in a relationship is in any way tied to your choice to be single, but a lot of people do, and more direct answers can cause them to feel offended. Responding this way shows you're not closed off to the idea of finding someone or putting yourself out there, but you just don't want to right now. And, assuming that you know the person you're talking with well, they will be happy that you're happy and will likely leave the topic alone because they just want what's best for you.

But from the people that know you best, there can come more dangerous comments. Comments like, "you're too picky," and questions like, "why can't you just find someone?" can really be hurtful, especially coming from someone like a parent or a close family member. The good news is, since you're likely very close with the person saying these things, you can be more direct and honest. It's usually more acceptable for you to say something like, "It's not that I'm picky, I just want to spend some time focusing on myself right now." The better you know the person, the more specific your answers can typically be. Just remember, the truth will set you free. But try not to be defensive. A calm answer comes from a place of comfort and happiness in your singleness, and how you respond conveys that to the people you're interacting with. If they pick up on how comfortable you are with being single and with getting those comments, they will likely accept your answers much more readily than if you seem taken aback or defensive.

One of the best ways to answer calmly is to soften your response with qualifiers such as, "for me," "right now," or "it's my preference." A lot of people respond critically to different perspectives because they feel as though you're judging them for not being like you, when in fact your decision has nothing to do with them. By adding any of those qualifiers, you're owning your singleness as a personal decision that you're not imposing on anyone else. It also helps your own mentality, which we'll talk about a little later.

At the end of the day, your relationship status is no one's business but your own. In Chapter 1, we talked about how to come to terms with being single and relearning how to look at your singleness. Keep that chapter bookmarked, or write down any key takeaways from that chapter and look at them often. Everything in this book is about a process that's uniquely personal and is meant to be customized to your own journey and mental health.

Chapter 4: It's Not You and It's Not Them

Stopping the search for the right someone before you've found them doesn't mean you have to ignore the signs if someone is put right in front of you. It just means that you're not scrolling through a dating app on your precious lunch break at work or staying out late with someone when you just feel like staying home and doing nothing. If a person crosses your path while you're not actively searching and you feel like pursuing them, go for it! But if it doesn't happen, there's no reason to feel guilty for focusing on yourself right now.

This chapter is especially for all those out there who tried the blind dating/dating app/singles group thing, and it just didn't work. Do you feel like giving up the search? Are you feeling guilty for not looking anymore, even though you haven't found your special someone yet? Keep reading—you'll feel better soon. Sometimes there are other areas of your life that need your attention, and that's okay!

In the first chapter, we talked a lot about what's causing you to want to stop actively looking for a partner and how to arrive at the decision to stop looking. We mentioned a lack of success in your searching as one of the primary causes of not wanting to continue putting yourself out there. This chapter deals a lot with that and gets deeper into figuring out how and why you stop the search.

There's no denying that it is hard to know when to stop playing the field. Dating around can be mentally and emotionally exhausting, not to mention time consuming. But what if it's worth it? What if the day after you delete that dating app, the perfect person would have come along? First of all, thinking about the "what if"s will drive you crazy. To put those thoughts out of your head and stay in the game one day longer than you think you should, just to prove to yourself that dating isn't for you, is a bad idea.

Another thing that helps is revising your self-talk to include the qualifier of "right now." So, instead of saying "dating isn't the right choice for me," try saying "dating isn't the right choice for me right now." By adding those two words, you're telling yourself that whatever came before those words isn't permanent. You're allowing yourself to change your mind in the future. Like we talked about in the last chapter, "right now" softens any statement and generally improves your attitude toward whatever came before those words.

Now, since we've covered approaching the *concept* of stopping dating, it's time to address the *actual decision* to put down dating. What are some of the signs you should give dating a rest? It's a little different for everyone, but some of the big warning signs are:
- You're tired after a conversation with every person you try going out with.
- You dread checking your phone.
- You feel guilty for leaving your date's message unread but you just don't have the energy to text them back.

- The past few people you've gone out with just haven't been right for you.
- The biggest hallmark sign: you tell yourself before every date, "I don't want to do this."

Any of these apply to you? Then you're in the right place. It's probably time for you to take a step back from dating...for now.

Having any of the above thoughts or feelings is completely normal, but it's also a sign of burnout. Burnout can be caused by a lack of balance in your life or just by throwing all of your energy at something for a long time with no results. To help narrow it down, try just calling it quits on dating for a while and see if you feel better. If not, it's a safe guess that, in addition to calling your dating life off for a while, you have some self-care to do.

If you're lucky, you haven't had reservations about putting down dating to focus on something else like your career or your own mental and physical health. And yes, that does make you lucky. You might feel like a bad person for breaking it off with someone because there aren't feelings there or you're just being pulled in too many directions right now. You might be feeling guilty for deleting that dating profile because you don't have the time or mental energy to keep up with it and everything else life is demanding of you.

If you haven't heard it yet, remember that you are not a bad person for "giving up" on dating so quickly and deliberately. You know what's right for you at this moment in your life, and, like we talked about earlier, you can always add the "for now" to your statements—both to others and in your own mind. You aren't a bad person for putting yourself first and knowing where your priorities are.

Of course, if you're looking for affirmation to take that leap and get out of the dating game, make sure you also heed this word of caution: make sure that however you exit, be it breaking up with someone or just cutting off messaging people, you do it politely. Own your choice and try not to leave collateral damage that you'll feel guilty over later. Guilt is the enemy of happiness, and you'll find it hard to follow the rest of this book's advice if you feel guilty over being single.

If you've ever dated, you know it takes a lot of time and energy. And the balancing act between dating (especially looking for a partner) and your day-to-day responsibilities can be a lot to handle. When you're single, all that time and energy can start going to other things like self-care or your career. In your first few weeks of being single, or if you've always been single, in your first few weeks of trying the advice in this book, make a list of the parts of your life that you've been neglecting to make time for dating and see if there's something that you've been missing out on that you want to devote more time to.

A word of caution, though: don't immediately try to fill all the time you were spending trying to get a date with other activities. The best thing for burnout (and this goes for any aspect of your life) is to take it slow at first. When you're burnt out, you're really hurting for some free time and some low-stress activities until you can recharge your metaphorical batteries. Try going to bed earlier, watching a movie at night to unwind, or taking a few hours to get back into a hobby you miss. But whatever it is you decide to do with your newfound free time, do it slowly. Take time to savor it, even after you feel your energy come back.

Chapter 5: Investing Time Elsewhere: Family and Friendships Are Important Too

When you get out of a relationship, you have more time to nurture the other relationships in your life. As far as long-term investments go, investing in quality friendships, whether it's forging or maintaining them, is one of the best things you can do for yourself. Friends often stick around a lot longer than romantic relationships do, and the relationship style is very different.

If you're fortunate enough to have family that you're close with, keeping those relationships healthy is just as important as building and maintaining friendships. Your family has likely been strapped into your relationship journey longer than anyone else in your life, and they'll understand what you're going through. Having family around you, be it in person or digitally, will help you feel less alone in this period of adjustment as well as provide sounding boards for how to adjust to being single.

Chances are, someone in your family has been where you are before. To have someone there for you in person who has experience figuring out how to make it as a single person will be an absolute game changer. Now, of course, that can be said for friends as well, but an older family member adds a completely different perspective. Listen to them and their experiences trying to find a partner, dating, and knowing when to be single. Their experiences may not have involved the

Internet, but there are probably still some words of wisdom for you in the stories they have to share.

Another benefit of investing time in your relationship with your family is that family won't be around forever, and having the opportunity to share more time together is valuable. Even if your family is in a different country or region, just setting aside time to communicate with them and share life with each other will help you feel less alone and more connected to the outside world.

If reading those last few paragraphs made you feel sad because you're not close with your family or don't have them in your life, the idea of a found family might cheer you up. Found family is an idea in literature, but it's also a real thing in real-life relationships. "Found family" refers to what happens when your friend group becomes so close that you all feel like family. It's a good feeling to have and when your family of origin isn't in your life, having those close friendships really does help you get through life. That being said, building and maintaining those friendships take time as well.

Nurturing friendships doesn't take anything special or complicated. Quality time spent with friends will automatically strengthen your relationship over time. Being able to show up for your friends when they need someone is another thing made easier by being single, though it's a habit you and your friends should form even as you get into romantic partnerships in the future. Friends offer unique perspectives on your life that will probably help you in your journey to becoming fully comfortable and happy being single, as well as in many other aspects of your life.

You may be reading this and feeling down because you don't have a tight-knit group of friends that you can spend this time bonding with. Maybe you parted ways, or maybe you or they moved away and lost touch. Don't worry! Now is a great time in your life to make new friends. Yes, making friends can be just as mentally and emotionally draining as looking for a romantic partner, but you might be pleasantly surprised at how easy it is to click with the right person! Friendships tend to form in the most unlikely ways. In later chapters, we'll talk about some of the activities you might like to do as a single person, and any one of those might be where you meet your friends and find your community.

Community is another important concept to pay attention to. More than just friends, having a community of people that you support and that you know will support you is so important in this time of change in your life. Many communities are formed around a shared activity, interest, religion, or geographical location. You might find a community at a class, at the gym, online via social media, or somewhere you frequent regularly, like a coffee shop. Keep your eyes and heart open, and you'll be surprised at what you find!

No matter what people tell you, you can actually make friends on the Internet. It's not the same friendship as you might have with someone you can see in person and do activities with, but having virtual friends in other parts of the world or your own country will really help to bring different perspectives into your life and broaden your horizon. Also, if you're just chatting with them on social media, you probably don't have to care if you look like a mess! It really is the little things...

However your community takes shape, you will find friends and a group of people you feel you belong with eventually. It's hard to come out of your shell after a bad romantic experience, but you can do it, and you'll be rewarded for your patience. Don't feel bad if you don't click with someone immediately. Good things come to those who wait, and you'll find your people eventually.

Once you have your friendships, you'll be far better equipped to tackle big changes and challenges in life. Having a support system and people to regularly spend time with will do wonders for your ability to handle stress, and it will make you feel better when life gets hard. You'll also be able to do some good in the world by supporting your community when they need it.

Part II: How to Be Single: Being Truly Happy and Comfortable When You're Single

We mentioned that all-important free time more than once in the last few chapters. It's easy to paint a rosy picture of having all this free time and being able to fill it with things so you feel recharged. That's all well and good, but what if you just got out of a relationship and are not only having to readjust to being single but now have voids left from when you did things with your partner? That last chapter may not have been as meaningful to you because you're still trying to figure out how to make that adjustment before you can even think about what you want to do in your free time. This section will be a lot more beneficial to you if you're coming from a recent relationship.

This next part is all about what you can do to enjoy being single and to make the best of times that used to be earmarked for hanging out with your partner. We'll talk about things like getting to know yourself, Friday nights as a single person, and how to fill your weekends in ways that don't leave you bummed out because you're not in a relationship. The whole idea behind these next three chapters is to help you think of things to do that are fun for you, so you feel like you're not missing anything by not having a significant other. When someone asks you what you did last weekend, your answer isn't "nothing." (Unless you want it to be.)

Of course, you don't have to fill every second of every free hour with an activity or something productive. If you just want a weekend of doing absolutely nothing, go for it! Listening to your mind and body will get you so much farther than following every suggestion you read in a book.

Before we dive in, it's important to note that this section is in no way a to-do list or an instruction manual that you have to follow to the letter. There will be things in here that aren't up your alley or just don't apply to you. Don't force something you don't want just so you can follow all the advice in this section. We're also going to talk about mental health, which varies for everyone, so make sure you read through the next chapters with your own journey and goals in mind.

Chapter 6: It's About More than Just Physical Energy

Energy has been mentioned a few times so far, but what does it really mean? And what, exactly, does it mean in the context of relationships? Physical energy is pretty easy to understand. Other components of your overall energy levels are mental and emotional energy. It's all hard to measure and requires you to be in tune with yourself. Listening to your gut feelings and living a balanced life will keep your energy levels up in all areas so you can keep enjoying life.

Burnout

Hopefully you've never experienced total burnout before. Burnout happens at a lot of jobs when you're overworked and stressed constantly, and you can't enjoy a beneficial work/life balance. Burnout doesn't just come from jobs, though. In fact, it may have been burnout that caused you to give up the search for a romantic partner and start reading this book. You can get burned out on any activity you do frequently without an adequate break.

What can you do to avoid burnout? Take regular stock of your mental and emotional energy levels to see what you have energy for after you're done with the things you have to do for the day. You can also try changing up your routine and taking breaks from activities that require a lot of energy every day. Even generally, taking breaks can really help burnout.

Breaks can come in the form of not eating lunch at your desk or even taking a day off every once in a while. If you feel burnt out on something that's not work, try taking a "vacation" from that task or activity. Especially if you're not being paid for your time, why burn yourself out if you don't have to?

Unfortunately, sometimes burnout can't be helped. So, how do you come back from burnout? The simple answer is rest. Take a day as soon as you can to just do nothing. Literally, nothing. This will recharge your mental and emotional batteries. This is the best and fastest way to pull yourself out of burnout, even if you still have to do the thing that caused you to burn out in the first place. For instance, if you're burnt out from work, take a weekend to just do nothing so you feel less burnt out when you go back to work on Monday. Then you'll be able to go into the new work week with more energy to help you handle whatever comes next.

Emotional Energy

Emotional energy is hard to quantify, even though we've all felt when we run low on it at some point in our lives. We expend emotional energy when we listen to someone else's problems, try to offer council, or do something that is emotionally difficult like having a hard conversation with someone. Feeling intense emotions also takes or generates emotional energy. Positive emotions typically leave you with more emotional energy than you had before, where negative emotions leave you feeling drained.

When you're running low on emotional energy, it's hard to deal with stress. Oddly enough, it's easy to respond more strongly to things when you're drained emotionally, even though those responses take more energy and aren't always the best approach. It's a hard cycle to break. This cycle also contributes to burnout and difficulty in relationships.

The good news is that emotional energy does come back pretty easily. To regain emotional energy, all you typically have to do is take a break from emotionally intense activities and interactions. Staying away from drama is helpful in regaining emotional energy, as is not consuming news for a little while. You can also release any pent-up negative feelings that have been draining your energy. You'd be surprised how much better you feel after you've had a good cry. Talking with someone you trust who can take on your emotional stress is also a good way of regaining some of that energy.

Mental Energy

Mental energy is the energy you use to think and process information. Students often experience low levels of mental energy after a lot of schoolwork, and even professionals are not exempt from the drain from work tasks. Mental energy affects burnout and your desire to learn and try new things. It also, in part, dictates the hobbies you engage in on any given night.

If you're running low on mental energy, odds are you're just going to want to watch TV or scroll through social media. There's nothing wrong with taking a mental break. Just make sure you're consuming media that will make you feel better, not things that will make you feel sorry for yourself. By taking care of yourself and your mental energy, you're already on the fast track to being happier and more comfortable overall, especially now that you're single.

Identifying Energy Drains

It's easy to know what your physical energy drains are. Identifying the mental and emotional drains in your life is harder but just as important, if not more so. By identifying the energy drains in your life, you can assess whether you can make any changes to prevent deeper issues from arising as a result of being out of energy for a long time.

Some common emotional energy drains are:
- Trying to find a romantic partner
- Toxic relationships, platonic or otherwise
- Drama, whether you're in it or just watching
- High-emotion situations
- Emotional whiplash
- Anxiety and other mental illnesses

That's quite the list, isn't it? And there may even be long-term stresses in your life that aren't on this list. Everyone has stress. It's not good for us, but it is a part of life and we can't expect to completely eradicate it from our world. The good news is that we can still be happy and comfortable in our lives even when we're stressed. The key to developing good coping mechanisms is to identify the big stresses in your life before you feel overwhelmed.

How to Regain Your Energy

The sections on mental and emotional energy touched briefly on things you can do to regain some of your energy, but what else typically helps? You'll know better than anyone what works for you. Go with your gut as long as it's not going to harm you in the long run. In other words, don't eat as a way of reducing stress, get blackout drunk every night, or do anything else that could hurt you. That's not what we're going for with this. What we're aiming for are healthy, sustainable strategies for regaining your energy. Most stresses in life are long term, so do your best to develop habits and practices that are sustainable.

The umbrella advice for regaining energy is reducing your stress, both internal and external. Mental stress can be controlled more easily than stress coming at you from things outside your mind (and potentially your control). So, focus on how to reduce your stress daily. This could be a self-care routine, watching a TV show that makes you laugh, calling a friend or family member, working out, journaling, or meditating. You have so many options to reduce stress that there's bound to be at least one out there that will work for you!

You'll find that when you're managing your stress and energy levels, even if nothing about your life or social situations have changed yet, you'll feel so much more comfortable and in control. Carry these practices with you into this period of getting used to being single. It will be an adjustment if you're used to being in a relationship or going out on dates to try to find the right person, but now you have the tools you need to be able to adapt to that change and enjoy being single much faster.

Chapter 7: Changing Your Brain

By now, we've all gotten the message: your mental health affects every part of your life. In recent years, the media has started showcasing the importance of mental health, and having honest conversations about what's going on in your brain has become more common and acceptable than ever. So, let's have a talk about what's going on inside that head of yours.

Changing the way that you think about being single will make a world of difference in how happy and comfortable you are with your relationship status. It's also one of the least time-consuming changes you can make to improve your outlook on single life. That's not to say it's easy, but it's the first step in the right direction. We know that mental health journeys are uniquely personal, so please take all of this in, and fit what works for you into your own journey to becoming the happiest you can be in the life you are living. One of the biggest obstacles to finding comfort and happiness in being single is the message the media throws at us every day about being in a relationship.

In this the age of technology, the media really does control the message about a lot of things, including love. Romance and dating make for excellent TV, but the thing is, having all the media we consume show us happy couples and unhappy singles really does change the way we think about our own situations. We've probably all seen that scene in the movie at least once where the two main characters fall in love and suddenly all their problems go away. All these plot lines are quietly reinforcing our belief that we need to be in a relationship to be happy. But that's not true, and by being aware of the bias in the media you're consuming, you'll do wonders for your own happiness as a single person.

So, how do we un-learn what we've been seeing in the media about love and dating? First, be aware of the bias of the media you're consuming. Second, try staying away from rom-coms and any media that makes you feel sad about being single or that tells you by example that you need a partner to be happy in life. Instead, try watching content by other single people and consume media that reinforces a positive outlook on single life. The media you consume really does affect how you think and feel, so this is an easy and very important thing to do to improve your mental health and change your brain.

Every time you take something away, it's good to replace it with something else. So, before you give up those rom-coms that you used to watch to make yourself laugh after a hard day, find a comedian you like or a YouTube channel of funny animal videos that will make you laugh. Odd suggestions, but you get the idea. Think about why you consumed that romance-centric media, and replace their functions with non-romance-centric media that still does for you whatever the old media did.

Challenge:

Before we move on, challenge yourself to live one full day without looking at any media that has to do with love. It's easy to start by doing this on a day you're busy already and wouldn't look at media often anyway, but try it again on a day when you're just hanging around the house and would typically watch a movie or read a book that perpetuates that message that you need to be in a relationship to be happy. In the voids left by media in your daily habits, try doing something active or a hands-on hobby that you enjoy such as cooking or crafting. Just give it a try for a day and see how you feel! (Good, right?)

While you're working on not feeding the mindset of relationship = happiness, it's also important to change the way you think about yourself. Your self-esteem can take a huge blow right after a breakup or after a long search for the right someone with less-than-ideal results. That's completely normal! So how do you stop feeling bad about yourself for not finding someone? Change the way you think about yourself. That doesn't mean ignoring facts and advice from those who know you well, but if you're worried that you're doing something wrong that's causing you to be single, try putting those fears to rest by talking to someone you trust or by replacing those thoughts with something else.

Changing the way that you think of yourself will affect so many areas of your life. You'll be surprised how much of an overall change you'll see after a few weeks with your new mindset. Self-talk is a huge part of changing the way you think of yourself. Words of affirmation, whether said aloud or written down, are a great tool to help you center yourself and start retraining your brain to think well of yourself, no matter the circumstance. Make this a daily habit. Make a list of positive things you believe to be true about yourself and mix in a few things you want to be true about yourself that you're working on, and phrase everything in terms of "I am" or a similar positive phrase. Some examples are:

- "I am healthy"
- "I am happy"
- "I am happy with my body"
- "I am in love with life"
- "I love myself"
- "I am wise"

It might seem daunting to try to come up with a list of affirmations, but don't worry! Whether you only start with a few or you use the list above, more will come to you. Find a time every day to recite or write these down for yourself and appreciate the ones that are already true, and use the affirmations as a daily reminder to work toward the few that aren't true yet.

Another tip for changing your brain is to change how you think about others; namely, past dates and partners. It's just as easy to be hard on other people as it is to be hard on yourself sometimes. So, afford people no longer in your life the same courtesy that you give yourself and try to work on reframing how you think of them and your interactions. If you keep thinking negatively about someone or harboring hard feelings toward them, it only hurts you in the long run.

This part may be hard to read, but it's a necessary word of caution: when you decide to be single for a while, it's easy to fall into the habit of being anti-dating and negative toward dating, relationships, and your past partners to the point of being damaging to your mental health. Just because you don't want to date doesn't mean there was necessarily anything wrong with all the people you've dated in the past, but putting things in the negative does seem to make things easier to give up. Just remember, holding on to negativity is only hurting you and keeping you from being happy as a single person.

Now, changing the way you think about your exes looks a lot different when you're coming out of a breakup. You probably have more healing to do when it comes to changing the way you think about your ex. So, be patient with yourself and understand that negative feelings are part of the healing process. Just make sure they fade with time and you're not harboring any unnecessary resentment for longer than you have to.

Changing the way that you think in any of these arenas takes time and dedication. It takes self-awareness and a willingness to reflect on your thoughts throughout the day. Understand that progress is not linear, and be easy on yourself. Also, know when to seek help or talk with a friend or someone you trust. Like we've talked about before, your mental health is something uniquely personal and only you know what's best for it, but the areas we've talked about here are great singleness-specific areas to target to help ensure your happiness. And remember, above all, you are responsible for your own happiness and comfort, and no one can give you that or take it away from you. You've got this!

A Quick Note on How to Adjust to Being Single

Now that you've got some background in stress, energy, and mental health, how do you apply all that to figuring out how to navigate life as a single person? Being comfortable starts with figuring out how to adjust to this new way of life. This note is for those of you who haven't been single for a while and aren't used to it. If you've been single for a long time, you're already probably a pro at adjusting to it!

The first few weeks after deciding to fully commit to being single will be a little rocky. That's not a sign to give up and start spinning your wheels trying to find someone. Just stick it out—things will get better.

In the coming chapters, we'll discuss some common roadblocks to your success as a single person, as well as give you some ideas about how you can use your time now that you're the only one who controls it. While you're developing these habits and learning what you like to do in your free time, it's helpful to have a few tips on how to handle this in-between time.

But first, a word of warning: these first few weeks are the ones where you're most likely to feel like you regret your decision. You're also the most likely to listen to anything that's shaming you for being single. This is the time, more so than any other point in your life as a single person, that you really need to take the advice in Part I of this book to heart. Be careful to only surround yourself with people who love you and support your decision, and be careful of the hidden messages in the media you consume. And before you give up and go back to the dating pool, wait a few weeks to be sure that it's really what you want, and that you're not just doing it because you haven't figured out what makes you happy about being single.

If you're more of an optimist, this may not be as much of a problem. You may already even have a list of things you've always wanted to do that you didn't make time for before, and you can't wait to get to it! If that's the case, good for you! You have it good, friend. Just make sure you're not repressing anything that's going to come out later and cause you to be unhappy at that time. Enjoy the quick transition to a comfortable and happy life as a single person!

If you're not quite that far into your journey yet, you're among so many friends. Most of us aren't that prepared when we're trying to figure out single life. So, make sure you've got your support group, your comfort activities, items, and food, and you allow yourself to feel however you need to feel. Mourn the loss of the idea that you're going to find a partner at this moment. Take some time to clean out records of past relationships and/or romantic interactions from your phone. Do whatever you have to do to feel like you're at a place where you can read through the rest of this book and see a beautiful new lifestyle for yourself.

No matter what you do to adjust, as you keep reading, look at all the advice presented through the lens of "will this activity/thought/perspective help me become happier and more comfortable?" If the answer is "no" or "I'm not sure," proceed with caution. It's super fun to experiment with how you spend your time and changing how you think is the mark of a mature person, but if you think it's going to hurt you or hinder your quest for comfort and happiness, then either don't do it, or stop doing it when you realize how it's affecting you.

Don't let this note discourage you! It's just a word of warning so the next chapters don't completely gloss over the adjustment period, painting everything in a much rosier light than they maybe feel to you right now. If you really want to see a light at the end of the tunnel, head over to the Extras section before you keep reading for some ideas of activities and hobbies you can do as a single person (without making it weird) so you know what you have to look forward to!

Chapter 8: Grow As You Go

Being newly single is a great opportunity to focus on your own development as a person. It's easy to let yourself fall by the wayside or pick up a few bad habits from past relationships and think you just don't have time to break them. Once you've got one less thing to worry about though, you'll have a little bit more time to focus on what about yourself you'd like to work on. That being said, as you're reading through the rest of this book, and as you think back on past chapters, consider your journey and what you'd like to change about yourself so you can grow as you go through this change in your life.

This chapter is not an invitation to be down on yourself, though. Acknowledging things you'd like to change about yourself and picking yourself apart for no reason are two wildly different things. Make sure when you're considering what you'd like to see change that you're backing it up with an action to help you be more kind to yourself. We all have things we'd like to change, and that's okay. Be patient with yourself and honest about what you'd like to change and how you can change it, and that will go a long way. You'll hear that a lot in this book.

Speaking of being honest with yourself about what you'd like to change, it's easy to see yourself through rose-colored glasses. It seems that those who are not hard on themselves may not always see things that they may want to consider changing. Again, that's not meant to offend, but it's sometimes the way humans work. Honesty is so important when it comes to changing yourself.

If you're feeling like you want a change but you can't think of what, if anything, you want to change, take a little bit of a closer look. Maybe your desire for change is because of something super small that's just been bothering you for a while but you didn't realize was a problem. Maybe it's a case of rose-colored glasses. As important as honesty is, patience is key as well. Understand that change takes time and even discovering what and how you want to change yourself is going to take time too. If you make a change hastily, you may live to regret it, or the change may not stick.

So, how do you grow as you go? If change takes time, it must also take energy, right? How are you supposed to focus on growth while you're trying to figure out how to be single, too? It's an interesting thing: you're growing by figuring out how to be happy as a single person. There are so many opportunities to grow as you go through this book, and you may not have even realized it! If you've just been reading through the book out of curiosity or without taking any action on what you're reading, feeling like you need a change or want growth is probably your sign that you should try reading through the book again and try out some of the advice. If you have been practicing what you're reading, keep it up! Your desire for change and growth will definitely be exercised in later chapters.

Despite this being a book on being single, there's more to growth than just regarding your mindset and your feelings about your relationship status. Personal growth can take so many forms. The messages of change that surround you every day can, as well. Inspiration and motivation for growth are always all around you if you look for them. Of course, it's important to recall what we've talked about regarding the media you consume as you consider the sources of your growth influence: *Only you know what kind of media is good for your mental health, so just keep this in mind when you're looking for a movie to watch on a Saturday night; and if you're already feeling a little down, maybe don't turn on that rom-com and find a good old-fashioned comedy instead.*

Despite the mention of a rom-com, the past chapter did have a point: only *you* know what kind of media is good for your mental health. If you're looking for a change and the media you're consuming is promoting drastic or unhealthy changes or habits, maybe now isn't the best time to consume that media. All of this is to drive the point home: evaluate your source when it comes to messages of growth! If you look to the outside world for how you can grow, consider your source. Is your source promoting something healthy: growth and habits that can last and make sense for your life? If you're talking with a friend or family member, it's probably safe to say you can trust their advice, but a little critical thinking is still nice.

As discouraging as these warning labels may feel, the desire for growth is good! Growth can take so many forms, and you'll be thankful you made a change now while the motivation is there. Forcing a change is never ideal, nor will it promote a successful growth rather than a short-lived behavior. So, be patient with yourself, and wait for growth to happen.

What does growing as you go look like, exactly? (All this abstract language is great, but what's the path forward?) Read this book critically. That's the first step. The process of reading this book and taking the advice to heart will prompt you to grow automatically. Another way to grow as you go through life is to make regular changes and try new things. We've used growth and change interchangeably in this chapter, but they are actually different. Growth is progress in the right direction to improve yourself, whereas change can be either good or bad. Changes can and do prompt growth if the changes are healthy things for you. Try new things! Grow through new experiences, both with people and alone, and listen to what the world is telling you.

Before we move on—the rest of this book is full of major opportunities to grow. Take notes if that helps you! Make a plan for trying new things (some ideas are down in the Extras section). If you're more internally-focused, make a list of things you'd like to change about yourself and figure out how to make those changes. Plan to grow and you'll grow as you go without even noticing! Your alone time, which we'll talk about next, will be instrumental in your success and growth. If you happen to have a specific growth goal in mind already, keep that in mind as you read on.

Chapter 9: Comfort in Alone Time

There's no denying it; when you're single, you do spend more time alone. It's time to get comfortable with it. Alone time is a good thing if you treat it right! Finding comfort in solitude has a lot to do with knowing yourself and finding balance. You don't have to fill every spare minute with activities or with other people, but you also don't have to spend all your free time alone. Balancing the two is something that will need some consideration and will change as you settle into your solitude. Your personality type will also definitely affect what happiness and comfort in alone time looks like for you.

For the introvert, odds are you're going to really enjoy your solitude. It's going to take some getting used to, but you're going to find happiness in your alone time much faster than others. Any change in routine takes some adjustment, so be patient with yourself, and you'll realize how much more relaxed and rested you feel at the end of every day that's not spent socializing with potential partners because you feel like you have to. Now, that's not to say that it's in any way recommended that you spend all your free time alone. Just pay attention to how tired you feel at the end of social interactions with different people, and decide when you have the mental and emotional energy to spend time with others. When you listen to yourself, you will feel so much more comfortable in your alone time because you know you're doing the right thing for you.

In place of when you would normally be going out on dates, do something restful for yourself, whether it's in the house, going out somewhere you don't usually get to go, or a combination thereof. Once you take back control of your time and aren't constantly having to rearrange your schedule to be able to go on dates in an effort to find or keep a partner, you'll have the time and energy again to enjoy the things you used to do by yourself to recharge. This is also a great time to work on that growth goal we talked about in the last chapter.

Just because you consider yourself to be an introvert doesn't mean you're expected to spend all your time alone. Maybe it's your preference to not spend a lot of time with people every day once you're done with your daily responsibilities, but it's also normal and encouraged to spend time with people every now and again. Just make sure that the people you're choosing to spend your time with are uplifting and overall fun to be around. Hopefully then you'll feel a lot less drained at the end of your social interactions.

And remember, moderation is important. Swinging from one extreme of how you spend your time to another isn't going to help you adjust to having free time. If your schedules allow, maybe have a designated time set aside to hang out with friends every so often so you all have something to look forward to. It's not like it has to be planned weeks in advance, but sometimes it's nice to know when you'll want to save a little mental energy up to really enjoy your social interactions. The same goes for extroverts, too.

If you're an extrovert, finding comfort in your alone time is going to be one of the greatest challenges of single life, but don't let that stop you! Odds are, if you're an extrovert, you also like having activities to do when you have a gap in your schedule. The good news is that alone time can be full of activities! Try making a to-do list of alone time tasks or activities that will help you feel recharged and take the edge off of not being out with someone. You can also call a friend or message with a family member on-and-off when you're not physically with someone to help take the edge off of your alone time. And even extroverts need some down time. You might find after trying a Friday night at home that you actually do feel better, and you didn't need to go out that night to be happy. You just didn't realize it! Alone time is a great time for self-reflection, wearing comfortable clothes, and doing whatever you feel like without worrying about someone else's needs.

When you're contemplating what to do with all your newfound free time, don't forget about your friends and family! For extroverts, spending time with people you know and love can be so much more rejuvenating than spending the day in. Having a group of people in your life that you find easy to be around and genuinely enjoy spending time with will make a world of difference in the way you think of your newfound free time.

If you've been reading this chapter and saying to yourself, "none of this quite sounds like me," don't worry. There are actually very few people that fall perfectly into "introvert" or "extrovert." Since we're all so unique, we all have different ways of rejuvenating ourselves. Some of your favorite restful activities will be extroverted, and some will be introverted. It's likely that you lean one way more heavily, but you shouldn't constrain yourself to one set way of being just because you want to fit into a box.

If you're in between introverted and extroverted, listening to yourself is extremely important. There will be some days that you feel like spending your free time alone, and some days when you actually genuinely do want to go out and spend time with friends or family. Of course, be mindful of the impact your choices have on others when it comes to last-minute decisions or cancelling plans, but go with your instincts as much as you can to find a rhythm that makes you the most comfortable in your alone time.

Chapter 10: "Alone" Doesn't Have to Mean "Lonely"

No matter your personality type, alone time is important, and it's equally important to know how to use it wisely. You will naturally feel more unhappy and lonely if you don't have things you genuinely enjoy to fill your time (because let's be honest, none of us feel on top of the world after mindlessly scrolling on our phones for three hours), and there's a reason for that. At some level (deeper for some of us than others), we all desire some measure of structure. Having a few activities, hobbies, or tasks you want to get done during your alone time will produce a much happier you than if you spend the entire day becoming one with your couch.

The key to this whole "alone time" thing is moderation. There's nothing inherently wrong with mindlessly scrolling through your phone, as long as you remember what we talked about in Chapter 4 about the kinds of media you're consuming, and make a conscious effort to consume media that doesn't make you unhappy with your life. Just listen to your body and mind, and know when enough is enough and it's time to get up and do something. We'll get into things you can do in your alone time in later chapters, but before we get there, start thinking about hobbies you've always been interested in picking up or that you used to do and miss. This will hopefully make you excited for your alone time and give you a few ideas on how to use it wisely.

Your attitude toward being alone and your past experiences being single or having a lot of alone time will also shape how you think about being alone and how you feel when you do have some alone time. Being alone does not have to mean that you feel lonely. "Lonely" is a feeling, but being alone is a state of being where there isn't anyone else in the room with you. You do have control over both of these, but loneliness is the easiest one to change.

So, how do you avoid feeling lonely when you've spent the day alone? Again, it's your mindset. That's the first thing. If you spend your time focusing on how alone you feel and how isolated you think you are, you will automatically feel lonely. It's also possible to literally make yourself lonely by believing you will be lonely. It's kind of a trippy idea, but it's true for more things than just convincing yourself that you're lonely when you may not be otherwise. It's the same psychological principle that causes you to feel hungry when you're actually not, just because you think you are or would normally eat at that time of day. It's amazing what your mind can control.

That got a little meta, but the point is, if you believe you will be lonely, you will feel lonely. So, honestly, the simplest thing you can do is to not focus on it. Instead, focus on what you're doing, the projects you're working on, or anything else that won't cause you to feel down. If it helps, put on a podcast or a YouTube video. You'll find that you actually enjoy being able to listen to whatever you want without interruptions.

Another way to avoid feeling lonely when you're spending time alone is to keep busy doing things for yourself - things that you'll benefit from. That could be self-care, cleaning, generally improving your environment, taking a nap, or spending time outside. There's a list down in the Extras section that might serve to provide more inspiration for you if you're looking to try something new during your next afternoon by yourself.

By choosing activities and projects that are distinctly for you and your own benefit, you're not only fending off loneliness by having something else to focus on, but you're also being intentional about your time and using it to care for yourself in ways that you may not be able to when you're with other people. Taking time out of your busy schedule to take care of yourself will improve your overall mood, decrease the chances of you being unhappy with your life, and help you look forward to spending more time alone.

It's also worth noting that loneliness is caused by the absence of connection, not the absence of people in your vicinity. Have you ever felt lonely at a party? Lots of high school and college-aged people have. There are so many people around, but are any of them your friends? Do you know any of them? Maybe not. And that's why you feel lonely. If you were at a bar with your closest friends, odds are you'd feel far less lonely because you have a connection with them. Ultimately, you're in control of what you think, even if it doesn't always feel like it (with a few notable exceptions if you struggle with certain types of mental disorders).

So, how does that tie in with alone time? When you're alone, especially if you're an extrovert, it's easy to convince yourself that you feel lonely right away; but if you feel like you have people you can talk to when you feel that loneliness creeping in, it'll come up a lot less often. And be that person for your other friends, whether they're in a relationship or on the singleness journey with you. Doing kind things for others is a great distraction from any of your problems, and you'll be glad for some social interaction yourself.

All that being said, if you're an introvert, you're far less likely to seek out social interaction, and this can cause you to get stuck in your own head. Have you ever had that feeling where you're not quite connected to the real world, and you didn't notice until a phone call or a text message snapped you out of it? That might be a sign that you need to spend some time with other people for a little while. In a less obvious form, you know you've had too much alone time when you stop wanting to spend time with other people altogether for a long period of time. Social isolation is not healthy, as we all know, and it's important to recognize that just because you're not in a dating relationship doesn't mean you have to be socially isolated. Know the signs of too much time alone and have people who you genuinely enjoy spending time with that you can seek out when you need some socialization. Just make sure it's reciprocal, too.

So what can you do with your alone time to take your mind away from anything that could cause you to start feeling lonely? The following chapters will offer plenty of suggestions on both the macro and micro level of occupying yourself. You don't have to do anything fancy or expensive to keep yourself from feeling lonely, nor do you even have to be doing something all the time.

We've talked a lot already about changing your brain, and it really does come into play here. How you think about your time and your perception of yourself has a huge impact on your happiness when you're alone. Having alone time is important, and so is what you do with it (and if you find yourself talking aloud to yourself when you're alone, you're not crazy—don't worry).

Hopefully this chapter leaves you feeling a little more relieved about the prospect of having more time alone. Of course, it bears mentioning that being single doesn't guarantee you any additional alone time, but it does increase your chances of making time for some additional alone time in your schedule if you so choose. That's why it's so important to know your personality type, how you like to spend your time, and what you like to do with your alone time.

Chapter 11: Joy in the Little Things

We've talked about comfort in Chapter 9, but what about happiness? Finding joy in the little things really makes a difference—not only for single people, but especially if you don't have a partner that you're going through life with regularly. Being single provides you the wonderful opportunity to capture the little things more often in life and to savor them at your own pace and in a way that is most meaningful to you.

Spontaneity is one of the greatest opportunities afforded to singles. A comedian once said that cancelled plans were like heroin in the sense that they give you an instant high, and that's absolutely true. You've likely felt it when plans got cancelled on that night that you just didn't feel like going out. As good as that feels, it also feels amazing to wake up one morning and say to yourself, "I feel like doing this today, so I'm going to do it." So, on the Saturday morning when you're feeling like shaking things up, take a moment to be thankful that you don't have to negotiate a plan with someone else or apologize to someone for not being available to them when they decide they want their spontaneous plan to include you.

By being single, you are now guilt-free and completely free to change your plans up or take on the day without a plan at all. If you're struggling to find joy in the little things, start there! Start with the knowledge that you have (within reason) total freedom and, in a sense, guilt-free ownership of all your free time. It's hardly a little thing, but spontaneity is certainly something to take joy in. At the end of the day, it's freedom that you're getting your joy from.

If you're someone who enjoys a little more structure and plans ahead for their days, make a list of things you've always wanted to do, keep it where you'll see it, and update it regularly. When you have the time, include something from that list in your weekend plans. It's a way to shake things up without causing yourself stress by going into your day with absolutely no plan.

There's also something to be said for having a plan and allowing yourself to throw it out the window. Stop somewhere different for lunch, stay a little longer at the mall, or go out to see a movie at the drop of the hat when you had originally planned to start that next project (which you can totally start later). As long as you're not hurting someone else or neglecting something that's necessary, sometimes just changing a small thing really makes a difference.

To that point, there's nothing like a day off from having a plan, especially if you're just tired and it's been a long week. Having a day where you just do nothing is different than being spontaneous in that there's rarely an activity and you're just trying to recharge your batteries. Being single means you don't really have to answer to anyone for why you're just taking the day to yourself, and that's something to certainly be happy about when you're looking at the pros of being single.

Turning off is also a very important part of recharging. Taking even an afternoon or evening off from being around your phone or computer can do wonders for your mood. It's a far cry from the anxiety we've probably all felt when we're away from our phones and someone we're seeing might text us and we'd miss it and offend them. As long as you're not in the middle of something or need to be connected to the outside world for some reason, try spending a few hours away from your phone guilt-free and enjoy it!

If reading's your thing, it's a good time to catch up on that book you've been trying to finish. If you have another offline hobby, having a phone-free period of time leaves you with little excuse not to get back into it. If all this sounds like fun but you really don't have anything that doesn't require the internet (or you just want to shake it up), the Extras section at the end of the book has a few lists of hobbies and activities that contain plenty of offline options. (You might want to get comfortable with the Extras! They come up a lot!)

Another great way to turn off and recharge yourself is to spend some time in nature. Spending time in whatever nature you have access to really helps you center yourself and reduce stress. This is more of an overall piece of advice for your mental health and wellness, but it's good to take extra care of yourself while you're adjusting to a new lifestyle. Fresh air is great for your health, and even just looking at real trees has been scientifically proven to improve your mood, reduce stress, and promote physical healing. If you have access to trees or a spot of nature of some kind (away from a big city if you can help it), try spending even a half an hour just walking among nature and focusing on what you're seeing rather than being stuck in your own head all the time or focusing on the negative things in life. If you're not able to take a nature walk, even just going to a courtyard with trees and plants and sitting and looking at them for a while really helps. If your workplace has some kind of nature nearby, that's a great place to take your lunch break, weather permitting.

Another little thing that makes you feel happier is exercising. Going to the gym after a long day of work is one of the best ways to release endorphins and make yourself feel better. Exercise is also a great form of self-care. It's a good way to get yourself out of the house or at least moving in some way. You should have more energy when you're done with exercising, and you will see physical benefits in addition to mental ones in most cases.

Exercise can take more than one form. You may not be in a place financially or physically where going to the gym is an option for you. Don't be discouraged! Going for a walk gets you outside and moving for free. There are also free videos online with no-equipment exercises for people of all fitness and mobility levels. The options are endless! And if sweating isn't your thing, you can still get moving without breaking a sweat. Try it for a week—you'll really like what exercising does for you.

If you want a challenge, try working out with a friend or setting a goal for yourself that you think is attainable. If you've always wanted to start working out but you don't really know where to start, you're intimidated, or you know you won't keep doing it consistently, maybe you should see a trainer a few times to get the party started. If you want the motivation and external pressure to keep going with your workout of choice (and can afford this), keep seeing the trainer or take a class regularly. Then you don't have to feel guilty for starting to work out and not continuing the habit.

If you're craving a little social interaction and maybe a challenge, try taking an exercise class at a gym or community center. The ones at community centers are often inexpensive, and if you're already a gym member, your gym may offer a wider variety of classes at reasonable prices to help you find what kind of class you're interested in. Classes are also a great way to make gym buddies or even friends if you frequent the same classes. Bonding with a pack of fellow enthusiasts makes working out much more enjoyable, and having a group of amateurs struggling along with you to master a new workout makes things a lot less awkward.

It genuinely is the little things every day that make a difference in your happiness. Hopefully after trying out a few of these suggestions, you can see for yourself the changes that making sure you do even one thing every day that makes you happy can bring to your overall comfort and happiness in life. And you can carry these habits and little joys in life with you even if or when you get into a relationship. You can share the benefits with your partner!

Chapter 12: Understanding Your Comfort Level

Before we move on, it's important to take a moment to pause and assess your comfort level with being single in the context of what we've learned so far. You've had a lot of information thrown at you, and it can be a lot to digest, especially if you're reading this over a short period of time.

Let's hit the high points of what we've reviewed so far, then we'll ask ourselves some questions to understand how comfortable we feel with being alone.

From Chapter 6:
Emotional energy is hard to quantify, even though we've all felt when we run low on it at some point in our lives. We expend emotional energy when we listen to someone else's problems, try to offer council, or do something that is emotionally difficult like having a hard conversation with someone. Feeling intense emotions also takes or generates emotional energy. Positive emotions typically leave you with more emotional energy than you had before, where negative emotions leave you feeling drained.

When you're running low on emotional energy, it's hard to deal with stress. Oddly enough, it's easy to respond more strongly to things when you're drained emotionally, even though those responses take more energy. It's a hard cycle to break. This cycle also contributes to burnout and difficulty in relationships.

The good news is that emotional energy does come back pretty easily. To regain emotional energy, all you typically have to do is take a break from emotionally intense activities and interactions.

On mental energy:

Mental energy is the energy you use to think and process information. Students often experience low levels of mental energy after a lot of schoolwork, and even professionals are not exempt from mental energy drain from work tasks. Mental energy affects burnout and your desire to learn and try new things. It also, in part, dictates the hobbies you engage in on any given night.

If you're running low on mental energy, odds are you're just going to want to watch TV or scroll through social media. There's nothing wrong with taking a mental break. Just make sure you're consuming media that will make you feel better, not things that will make you feel sorry for yourself for being single. By taking care of yourself and your mental energy, you're already on the fast track to being happier and more comfortable overall, especially now that you're single.

Also, it's good to keep this in mind about stress:

Everyone has stress. It's not good for us, but it is a part of life and we can't expect to completely eradicate it from our world. The good news is that we can still be happy and comfortable in our lives even when we're stressed. The key to developing good coping mechanisms is to identify the big stresses in your life before you feel overwhelmed...

The umbrella advice for regaining energy is reducing your stress, both internal and external. Mental stress can be controlled more easily than stress coming at you from things outside your mind (and potentially your control). So, focus on how to reduce your stress daily. This could be a self-care routine, watching a TV show that makes you laugh, calling a friend or family member, working out, or meditating. You have so many options to reduce stress that there's bound to be at least one out there that will work for you!

You'll find when you're managing your stress and energy levels, even if nothing about your life or social situations have changed yet, you'll still feel so much more comfortable and in control of your life. Carry these practices with you into this adjustment period of getting used to being single. It will be an adjustment if you're used to being in a relationship or going out on dates to try to find the right person, but now you have the tools you need to be able to adapt to that change and enjoy being single much faster.

In Chapter 7, there was a challenge. Did you do it? If so, how did you feel after? If not, give it a try:

Challenge yourself to live one full day without looking at any media that has to do with love. It's easy to start by doing this on a day you're busy already and wouldn't look at media often anyway, but try it again on a day when you're just hanging around the house and would typically watch a movie or read a book that perpetuates that message that you need to be in a relationship to be happy. In the voids left by media in your daily habits, try doing something active or a hands-on hobby that you enjoy such as cooking or crafting. Just give it a try for a day and see how you feel! (Good, right?)

While you're working on not feeding the mindset of relationship = happiness, it's also important to change the way you think about yourself.

Lastly, there were a few important tidbits in the note on adjusting to being single that bear repeating before we go into our reflections:

Now that you've got some background in stress, energy, and mental health, how do you apply all that to figuring out how to navigate life as a single person? Being comfortable starts with figuring out how to adjust to this new way of life. This note is for those of you who haven't been single for a while and aren't used to it. If you've been single for a long time, you're already probably a pro at adjusting to it!

The first few weeks after deciding to fully commit to being single will be a little rocky. That's not a sign to give up and start spinning your wheels trying to find someone. Just stick it out—things will get better.

But first, a word of warning: these first few weeks are the ones where you're most likely to feel like you regret your decision. You're also the most likely to listen to anything that's shaming you for being single. So this is the time, more so than any other point in your life as a single person, that you really need to take the advice in Part I of this book to heart. Be careful to only surround yourself with people who love you and support your decision, and be careful of the hidden messages in the media you consume. And before you give up and go back to the dating pool, wait a few weeks to be sure that it's really what you want, and that you're not just doing it because you haven't figured out what makes you happy about being single.

Now that we've recapped, let's figure out how comfortable you're feeling with the concept of being single. Take some time and consider your answers to the following questions and statements and, if it helps you, write down your answers. It might be beneficial to date your page if you do choose to write them down so that you can look back and see your progress a few months from now. Just answer the questions honestly and your answers will tell you everything you need to know. There are no "right" answers, only honest ones.

- Do you enjoy time alone?
- How long do you typically make it without talking to someone else before you feel like you're going crazy?
- Does it freak you out to be in a building alone?
- Do you feel like you need someone else there to validate you?
- When you think about what you're doing, do you typically frame your actions and perception of yourself in reference to what others think of you?
- Are you happier with people or alone?
- In this moment, do you miss dating?
- Do you ever think that you'll go back to dating?
- Is being single a temporary thing to you?
- How do you feel about developing a routine as a single person?
- Do you like change?

Now read or think back on your answers to these questions. How do you feel? If you answered positively to most of them and your answers indicated that being single is not a temporary thing for you, you're well on your way to becoming very comfortable as a single person. If you indicated that you don't like change and that you miss dating (alone, these answers are normal—it's just when they're together that they become significant), you've got a little work to do before you're ready to even consider being comfortable alone. If you're at the point where you want to be comfortable being single, try going back to Part I and taking a look at how to really get your mindset geared toward being single and making the most of it. Another thing you can do is keep reading with an open mind and see if reading through all the great benefits of being single changes your perspective a little bit.

If not, maybe it's time to consider getting back out on the dating field. That might seem like a radical suggestion, but if you have a good idea that you're not interested in becoming comfortable as a single person, why do something you know isn't comfortable? Honestly, maybe this was the only nudge you needed!

If you're already feeling more comfortable with being single, congratulations! You've learned a lot from the past two sections of this book and your mind is probably even more at ease after having answered these questions. The coming parts of the book will hopefully inspire you to make the most of your time and maybe try something new.

Maybe your answers weren't so illuminating. Not to worry; figuring out how to be comfortable being single is a process, and you'll get there eventually. And you can always re-read this chapter for a quick refresh on some things you can do to become more comfortable being single if you're feeling a little less settled than you'd like to be. It's probably best to take a look at what's making you feel uncomfortable and try to fix it before you get any deeper into the book; that way you can more easily follow the advice and can enter into this new phase of your relationship by being single with an open mind.

Part III: How to Be Single: Do What You Love and Love What You Do

We've covered how to be single in the abstract, in terms of your mental health, and in the relationship to your perception of your free time. Now, let's expand on your free time. In past chapters, having activities and things to look forward to has been mentioned a lot, but what does that look like? Where can you find ideas for what to do to take full advantage of your singleness and free time?

In all reality, there are so few times in our busy lives that we allow ourselves to do what we love, and sadly, it's rare to have a day where we love everything we're doing. So when you have that free afternoon and have the opportunity to do what you love, how will you spend it?

Ideas are all around you! Odds are, you already have a few somewhere in the back of your mind that you've been putting off because no one else wants to do them with you. Being single is a great excuse to do those things alone. You don't have a partner around to judge you or give you a hard time for not spending your weekend with them. Go do that activity or visit that weird restaurant you've always wanted to!

If you've got more ideas than you can ever reliably remember (come on, we've all been there), write them down! Make a list of everything you can think of that you've always wanted to do and keep it somewhere you'll see it often; maybe even put it on nice paper or a dry-erase board so you can update it when you get your next idea. Of course, you know your limits (financial, time, travel means, etc.), but if you keep thinking reasonably when you're making your list, you'll have something to come back to when you're feeling like you need to shake things up, but you just don't have the creative energy to come up with something totally new.

But if you're sitting down to make that list and the blank page has been staring back at you for a solid few minutes and you still can't think of anything (maybe you need coffee), read on, dear reader, for more adventure ideas! If you're looking for something now (and haven't gone over there already), hit up the Extras section for those lists to help you kickstart your own!

Chapter 13: Me Time

We've talked about the all-important time alone. We've covered how the ratio of time with people vs. time alone changes for introverts and extroverts. But how do you figure out what, exactly, you want to do with your "me time"?

The first piece of advice is to take some time to get to know yourself. Listen to your body and mind and what you really feel like doing. Especially after you get home from work, ask yourself (and answer honestly) "what do I feel like doing now?" After a few weeks of asking yourself this question, the answer will likely give you some insight on what you typically need to relax and unwind. As long as those answers are healthy for your body, mind, and budget, start making those activities into a routine and a set of habits that make you feel rested, recharged, and ready to face the next day. Being single affords you the opportunity to do this without worrying about how someone else fits into your plans. Take full advantage of it!

If you're wondering what might be considered healthy and sustainable answers (or if you feel weird talking to yourself to figure out what you want to do), here are some things that might help you unwind after a day at work:
- Go to the gym or work out at home
- Watch a funny TV show or video online
- Cook a more time-intensive dinner for yourself
- Clean something that's been driving you crazy for a few weeks

- Call a friend and chat
- Spend some time on a hobby or project you've been working on—there's nothing like working with your hands!
- Take a nap
- Plan what you want to do on your next day off
- Check in with your family
- Reorganize something
- Spend some extra time on personal grooming
- Journal

Hopefully some of those gave you a few ideas of what you could do that doesn't cost a lot of money or do you any physical damage and will help you unwind after a long day. This is not a to-do list, and if something on this list just isn't for you, then by all means do what makes you feel rested. These ideas are just something to help you get started on a list of your own.

A few things on that list bear highlighting, like personal grooming. Having a self-care routine is extremely important for building and maintaining comfort and happiness. If you don't feel like you're taking good enough care of yourself, you're not going to feel very happy. If you don't take care of yourself physically, odds are you're not going to feel very comfortable in your own skin either (it's hard, but we've all been there).

There are YouTube videos plastered all over the internet showcasing hours-long self-care routines that cost a boatload of money and require specific (and expensive) equipment and products. That's not necessarily what we're talking about here. If it's within your means to do something of that scale, go for it! For most of us, it's absolutely not, and our hard-earned money and free time is better spent elsewhere.

That being said, having a solid, reasonably priced self-care routine that fits your schedule is so important. And it might look different on different nights, so it might benefit you to develop a few routines that take different amounts of time so you have something you can do when you only have a few minutes and for when you have a few hours to really pamper yourself. Make sure you have a few things you see as a treat for yourself that you can do at home for those days when you just don't have a lot of time. If there are things that you like to do to take care of yourself outside of the home, such as getting your nails done or getting a massage, those might be better left for a day when you have more time.

For any length of a routine, skincare is one of the easiest ways you can take care of yourself. We should all have a skincare routine of some kind in place. It doesn't have to be elaborate or expensive. Drugstore products often work just as well as luxury brands. Find some products that work well for you and that you don't feel guilty about spending your money on. If you don't find that process frustrating, it can be its own form of self-care, because you're investing time in yourself.

Investing time in yourself can look different than just skincare and superficial maintenance. Exercising (yes, it's coming up a lot—it's one of the best things you can do for yourself!) and eating healthily are also great ways to practice self-care on the inside. We've talked a lot already about exercise in past chapters, but eating healthy foods is a new one. Making a healthy meal is an act of self-care. When you're in a relationship, it's pretty common to just eat whatever your partner is eating, and a lot of times, we gain weight when we're in a relationship and develop some questionable eating habits for recreation (unless you're dating a fitness junkie, that is). There's no shame in that, and the point of this is not to make you go on a diet or anything dramatic! It's just something to be aware of and another element of self-care you can explore on your quest to find the routine that works best for you.

If you like cooking, this will probably be easy for you. If you're not a fan or don't know how to cook very well, there are so many subscription services out there that will send you all the ingredients you need and the recipes for healthy meals. If you don't want to spend the money, turn again to the wonderful YouTube! There are a plethora of cooking videos that are designed for people looking to get into cooking, even if you have a dietary restriction!

All that being said, be sure that whatever you do for self-care isn't breaking the bank and that you don't feel guilty for doing it multiple nights a week. As we've talked about before, guilt is the enemy of being happy and comfortable and the whole point of self-care is to promote those positive feelings. Go easy on yourself and find fun and long-term ways to take the best care of yourself that you ever have in your life! Now's your time!

Speaking of food, another nice thing about "me time" is being able to grab a snack and watch a movie. It's a lot cheaper and easier to keep food in your freezer or pantry that's a special treat for you (as long as you know you have the self-control not to get into it regularly—keeping things in the freezer is great for that!). Treating yourself with food in moderation is just as fun as doing a more in-depth personal grooming routine. So come up with a few things that you consider a special treat, even if they're not the best for you, and keep them on hand for when you want something different. Odds are these special foods are going to be less than healthy. Don't beat yourself up for that—no one's ever heard of kale being a special treat! Just make sure you're not eating your feelings. That's not what we're talking about with self-care. Everything in moderation! "Cheat meals" and fun movie snacks are a perfect way to treat yourself at the end of the work week, and now you don't have to share unless you want to have some friends over to join you!

"Me time" doesn't necessarily need to involve being at home. If you want to broaden your horizons, you could take a class on something you're really bad at or have always been curious to try. Not everyone finds learning fun, nor does a classroom environment foster comfort and happiness for everyone, but the good news is there are so many ways to take classes these days that there's something out there for nearly everyone!

If you like in-person classes, community centers, local colleges, and some businesses offer classes on crafts, cooking, and art. These classes are sometimes free, but often cost a small amount for a few classes. There are usually courses for different skill levels, but beginner level classes are the most common and you'll be surrounded by people who are trying something new just like you!

If attending a class in person just doesn't work with your schedule, there are plenty of platforms online where you can take either live or pre-recorded classes for free or a small fee. Platforms like Skillshare are subscription-based sites that offer thousands of pre-recorded classes for all skill levels for a monthly fee. For those of us who aren't crazy about paying for yet another subscription, YouTube is always a great option. It's harder to find tutorials that are skill-level specific on the great wide Web, but there are lots of cooking and crafting tutorials out there. There are also plenty of individuals that have live classes on more niche topics that you could also track down via the Internet.

And if classes in general aren't your thing, consider trial and error to help yourself improve, or some self-guided research. Learning this way encourages your curiosity, allows you to learn at your own pace, and provides you a lot of laughs along the way! A self-guided delve into a new hobby is also a good way to see if you even like the activity before you invest too much time or money into it, and you can walk away at any time.

Another fun way to spend an evening is journaling. Especially if you're of the creative type, journaling is an excellent way to center yourself, get your thoughts organized, and express some creativity. If you're interested in journaling but you're not sure where to start, check out the extras at the end of the book for some prompts to help get you started.

Content aside, if you're on social media at all, you may have seen something called a bullet journal. Bullet journaling is a creative from of journaling that involves taking a blank book of your choice and designing your own pages. Some people use bullet journaling like planners with customized calendar spreads to help them stay organized. Some use bullet journaling as a way to write their thoughts down on a creative background. You can include whatever you want in these pages—photos, artwork, newspaper clippings, whatever brings you joy. A bullet journal can serve as a functional craft and an outlet for your creativity. Keep bullet journaling in mind when you get to the extras section about travel journaling as well—it's a nice concept for when you want a more flexible journal.

Like anything, bullet journaling can be as expensive and involved as you'd like it to be. All you really need is a blank book and a pen, but you can always go up from there in time commitment and materials cost. One quick Google search will provide you with many craft supplies and ideas to explore for yourself. That's what the weekend is for!

Chapter 14: Welcome, Weekend!

It's the weekend! Congratulations on surviving another week of the daily grind! As much as we all celebrate having a few days' break from our normal weekday obligations, as a newly single person, it's easy to dread the weekends. If you're coming out of a relationship where you used to spend every weekend together, weekends may not feel like something to celebrate…yet. Cheer up! By the end of this chapter, you'll be more excited for your weekends than you ever thought you could be!

Out on the Town

The first thing to talk about is going out on the town at night. If you're someone who enjoyed going out to clubs or bars, you don't have to give that up just because you're single. You just have to be a little more careful if you're flying solo (safety first, folks!). If you're not crazy about going out alone, take a friend or two and make it a party. If you feel like going out alone, make sure you're being careful and use common sense, and you'll still have a great time!

Going out on the town during the day is a far less complicated topic. While a shopping day with friends is a fabulous way to spend a Saturday, there is a particular joy in hitting the mall alone and getting to go at your own pace. It may sound lonely and like a great way to highlight that you're single, but it's really not all that uncommon. It's actually really fun! It also makes shopping for birthdays and holiday gifts much easier if you have that comfort level in place by the time those events roll around. Then you don't have to try to hide your purchases!

Speaking of comfort levels, it's worth noting that you might feel a little awkward going out on the town alone to any destination at first, be it an amusement park, the mall, or out for an activity. If you haven't picked up on it yet, a theme of this whole book is patience with yourself and trust in the process of acclimation, so it won't be a surprise that this, too, will take some getting used to. But you really will become so much more comfortable going out on the town alone after only a few times. And if it helps you get through any super awkward moments, call or text a friend so it looks like you're "with" someone, or keep earbuds in so no one bothers you (this one's especially helpful for all you introverts out there—you've probably already heard it a thousand times, though!).

Table for One

You may have noticed that we didn't include restaurants and going out to eat in the "out on the town" discussion. Going out to eat is such a point of contention for singles that it really did warrant its own section. You've probably encountered some stigma around going out to a sit-down restaurant alone at some point in your life, either from the media or through personal experience (hopefully not, though). Whatever your experience with the much-critiqued eating alone at a restaurant, hopefully you find some encouragement here. There's a lot you can do to feel less awkward eating out alone. Read on for advice on some of the most common hang-ups of eating out alone.

Your chosen environment is one of the biggest impacts on your comfort level of eating out alone. If you're at a restaurant that specializes in date nights and anniversaries, you're probably going to feel so much less comfortable than if you went to a pub or a more casual restaurant. The environments of more casual restaurants and ones that don't specifically boast romantic settings and menus are much more welcoming and laid back. You're also likely to spot a few other people eating alone if you keep your eyes out. If you're craving a more high-end experience, going to a restaurant in a hotel is a great idea as well. Lots of people travel alone and eat at whatever restaurant the hotel has for the sake of convenience, so you'll be among other single people.

A word of warning on restaurants with bars, though: a lot of other singles advice says to eat at the bar if it's offered because then you don't have an empty chair across from you. And while that sounds like great advice, be careful about sitting alone at a bar in an environment you don't know well. A single person sitting at a bar gives off a wildly different energy than the exact same person sitting at a table. For some reason, bars are inherently more social spaces, and if you're alone, you might get approached by at least one person while you're trying to enjoy your meal. If that's your thing, then the bar is perfect for you! If you don't want to talk to anyone and just want to enjoy your meal, a table will be a better seating option for you. Typically, strangers don't go up to peoples' tables to chat.

So, if you're sitting at a table alone, what do you do to make it less weird (especially while you wait for your food)? Depending on the restaurant setting, you might be able to get away with using your phone for entertainment. It's not for phone calls, but for scrolling through social media, catching up on texts, or for playing that game you just can't make time for during the week. If it's a more casual restaurant, you might even be able to bring earbuds and stream something if you want to. That might kill your vibe at the restaurant, but it's up to you how you like to enjoy your food. You could also bring a book if you're a big reader or a notebook if you prefer drawing or writing—something you enjoy doing and that will make you happy to be there. If you're in a more crowded establishment, people watching is also a great way to entertain yourself if you don't want to bring anything to do. Sometimes it's just nice to enjoy your meal without multitasking, and people really do provide endless entertainment.

The Staycation

If you don't feel like going out, or you're not able to that weekend, you can always plan a staycation for yourself. If you haven't heard the mid-2000s-born term before, a "staycation" is a period of time where you do something fun and different at home so you feel like you're on vacation without leaving your home. A staycation doesn't have to be elaborate or expensive and can be absolutely anything you want it to be! Head to the very end of this book for a longer list of ideas and where you could find more inspiration, but the highlights are spa days, movie nights, craft or hobby days, cooking days, and (weather permitting) gardening days. You could also re-create something you loved about an actual vacation you took such as the scents, an environment, or a food item you absolutely loved.

The point of the staycation is less of what you do during that time and more about how you feel. Staycations should be designed to make you feel rested, rejuvenated, and like you just went on a vacation—without the high price tag. Staycations can be as glamourous or as casual as you want them to be and don't have to take your entire weekend up if you don't want them to. Maybe it's just one of your days off and you stay in bed or on the couch all day watching movies or catching up on TV shows, and it's your excuse to actually have food delivered instead of making yourself go out and get the food. Whatever feels like you're on vacation!

They're also kind of fun to put together and plan out beforehand. You can get that pre-vacation buzz and you have something to look forward to, which is part of the benefit of a vacation. You also don't have to have a staycation alone. If you have close friends or family members that you really enjoy spending time with, you can always make it a group thing at your place or help a friend plan it at theirs. You can still have a theme or do whatever you want to, but sometimes it's fun to share the experience with someone.

The Day Trip

Feel like a real change of scenery? Try a day trip somewhere different! Even if it's just a quick drive a few towns over to a different shopping plaza or hiking trail, a change of scenery is sometimes welcome. If you live in a larger city, see if there are any buses or trains that run to other major cities that aren't too expensive. Amtrak and Greyhound run dozens of lines connecting major cities and there are sometimes decently inexpensive options for short-distance trips. Public transit is a great option if you don't have a car, want to go to a city that has expensive parking, or just don't feel like driving. It can also be an adventure in and of itself!

As much as we sing the praises of mass transit, if you don't live in a big city or just don't like mass transit (which is totally valid), road trips are a lot of fun! They're romanticized in books and movies for a reason! Turn on the GPS and a killer playlist and just cruise for a few hours down the open road. Unless you find driving super stressful, this is a great way to spend a sunny weekend day! If you live in a place where the next town is a decent drive away, maybe this is your sign to go explore it. Find a restaurant or shopping plaza that you want to check out and set your GPS! You're bound to have as much fun along the way as you do when you get there. And one of the joys of road tripping alone is that you can stop whenever you want and you don't have to worry about anyone else. If you see a roadside sign for an attraction that piques your interest, head on over! Why not?

If you're somewhat new to your area, day trips are a fantastic way to discover many fun places and activities that don't take too long to get to, but provide enough of a change of scenery to feel special. Even if you've lived where you do for years, you can still check travel sites for fun new activities that may have slipped under your radar.

Festivals are huge attractions during the spring and summer in a lot of areas, and they are often out a little ways from a major city and could be a super fun road trip destination. The good thing about festivals is that they're often so packed that no one will ever know you're there alone and, even if they did, they really won't say anything. You also might make a few friends along the way! Festivals are also not typically very expensive to get into and have lots of food and fun things to check out to make the drive well worth it. You might find that you really enjoy the festival and make it an annual destination.

No matter where you're driving, there's bound to be something that'll make the trip well worth the time and gas money. And there's nothing that says you have to plan it in the first place. If you're a wandering spirit, just pick a highway and start driving. A road trip alone can really be whatever you want it to be. The same goes for a day trip via mass transit. Get off at whatever stop you want, keep an eye out for signs, and go wherever you want. Just make sure you don't miss your ride home!

Nothing Like a Job Well Done

Another weekend activity that helps you capitalize on being single is tackling a big project that you've been meaning to get done but didn't make the time for when you were in a relationship. We've all got them, ranging from finally planting that vegetable garden to cleaning out your closet and reorganizing it.

Maybe your project takes you out on the town to pick up some things. This is always fun when you have an objective, and it can get you a little change of scenery before you get back to your project. It is truly satisfying to complete a project, and you'll thank yourself when you don't have to do it down the line. Capitalize on those weekends you feel like being super productive, and try to tackle a larger project.

It helps to keep a running list of projects you'd like to tackle when the mood strikes. We mentioned in earlier chapters keeping a list of things you'd like to do for ideas on days off. This list can live right next to that one for an inspirational little area (digital or in real life) for when you have a day off and feel like doing something.

Of course, projects don't have to take up your entire weekend if you don't want them to. You also don't have to do them alone—including some friends or family can really liven up the process, if not make it more efficient. You'll definitely make some memories along the way!

Friendly Competition

Lots of people played sports at some point in their childhood. Sometimes it's fun to revisit the sport you loved as a child now that you're a little older. And honestly, it's nearly impossible to be awkward as a single person when you're playing a team sport. The focus is the game itself, and you'll feel comfortable in no time. It's a good way to make friends, as well.

Competing is also proven to distract you from most things you're anxious about and provide you with an adrenaline high that will make you feel better. Just make sure you keep it friendly!

Most cities have amateur teams and groups for adults who enjoy sports and still want to play later in life. Lots of these are organized online with the help of social media and/or local community centers. These groups can range in seriousness (and therefore financial investment) from pickup game-style to full on leagues.

Whatever your taste in activities, there's a weekend pastime out there for everyone! It may take some effort to figure out how you like to spend your time, but knowing what your options are and seeking out some new things to try will get you well on your way. This book provides a few options and broad categories of things you can do for your weekends (check out the Extras for more), but the internet and any social groups you may be a part of will have countless more options for you to try something new. No matter what it is, make sure you're having fun.

Chapter 15: Have Time, Will Travel

Traveling: it's one of the luxuries in life. You can enjoy it even if you're not in a relationship. If you have the means, try taking a trip by yourself—it's the conglomeration of everything we talked about last chapter, so try those things first and build your comfort level before investing time and money in a trip that you think you might be uncomfortable taking.

Traveling alone is a lot of fun, but there are always things to take into consideration if this is the case. Make sure you're aware of your surroundings, and pick a destination that's pretty safe and well-populated. Let someone know where you are and when you're supposed to be back, even if they're not with you, so you have some accountability just in case. If you're curious about tips and tricks for safe travels alone, head to the Extras section at the end of the book for some additional advice. None of these warnings are meant to dissuade you from seeing the world alone if you want to, but they do bear mentioning.

One of the benefits of traveling alone is the freedom to do whatever you want when you feel like it. It can be so much more relaxing to get away by yourself to explore things that other people in your life aren't as curious about. You can also enjoy some scheduling flexibility if it's just your schedule you're working around. We talked about spontaneity a few chapters ago, and it really does come into play here. It's not always a wise financial decision to drop everything and fly somewhere for a week, but if you know you've got some time off coming up, try to take that time when flights are cheaper to head to a destination of your choice. There are so many options for vacationing on a budget. There's plenty of resources over in the Extras section if you're curious.

Money can become less of a damper on your wanderlust if you save up for it. Even if you don't have a trip in mind, setting aside even a little bit of money every month for when you want to get away makes it easier to just pick up and jet off somewhere for a few days, especially when combined with a few budget-friendly hacks. And the good thing is you will be used to being without the money when your friends want to plan a cruise or something more financially involved, and you'll be able to set it aside easily. Not everyone is in a place financially where they're able to do this sort of thing, and it's not really advisable to try if you know you're not making a sound decision, so caution is always advised. But if you can, try to earmark even $50 a month for travel—it really can go a long way every so often!

If you're not keen on traveling alone, find a travel buddy—someone who shares your interests and who you love being around and can have fun with. Maybe it's a family member or a good friend. Having someone along with you is a lot safer and often times less expensive if you're splitting things like a hotel room and cab fare. And on a less practical note, it's not necessary but it's really nice to have someone to share experiences with.

Traveling is a good way to get a change of scenery and prevent burnout in both your personal and professional lives. If you're the type that likes to have activities booked when you travel, check out the travel section of the Extras to find some resources for activities and experiences all around the world. There are even some geared toward singles! If you were thinking going in that you'll be judged for doing any activity alone, hopefully you've come to see how you can absolutely enjoy anything the world has to offer when you're alone.

So, whether you're with friends or by yourself, how do you plan a safe trip (especially on a budget)? The biggest thing to think about is where you're staying. We all know the reputation of cheap hotels. There's a lot of truth to the bad reputation, unfortunately for your wallet. Fortunately, in the hotel industry, there does come a point where money doesn't buy safety anymore, it just buys amenities. So, decide what amenities you care about and how much time you think you'll be spending at the hotel. If amenities aren't super important because you'll be out exploring most of the time, a mid-priced chain hotel with good reviews will probably be perfect for you. If you're traveling for the experience of staying at a high-end hotel, still read reviews, but the amenities are the main attraction for you. No matter what, read reviews!

In that same vein, look at the surrounding area of the hotel. If you're unfamiliar with the area, read the reviews of the nearby establishments and do a little Google Satellite stalking to get an idea of what the neighborhood is like. There's nothing worse than paying more for a hotel that's still in a bad neighborhood where you feel nervous even waiting for a cab outside.

That being said, look at transit methods as well. It might not be the wisest to attempt public transit in a city you're not familiar with. It's usually a good idea to stay close to the things you want to do, but it's unlikely you'll be centrally located to all the activities you have planned. Look at walkability (check the neighborhoods first!) or plan to take a cab or rent a car. Yes, these things do add cost to the trip, but there are always deals and discount codes for transportation. Just make sure you're using a reputable car rental company if you choose to go that route.

Now that you're all excited to travel, the final question is: where are you heading off to? Picking a destination can sometimes be super easy, but it's a little different when you're single. If you're just getting out of a relationship, try to avoid places that will make you think about your ex. If you're still struggling with adjusting to being single or coming to terms with it, avoid notoriously-romantic places unless you're with other single friends—then you'll forget all about not being in a relationship! The key to being happy and comfortable as a single traveler is all about environment. Pick a city that has a lot of attractions for singles or at least doesn't market itself as a city designed for couples.

If you're looking for the ultimate comfortable getaway (and maybe this requires less travel than you thought), book a room at a hotel/spa and just get pampered for a night or two. That's the height of luxury and if you're going alone, there's no one there to interrupt your relaxation. It's the ultimate singles' trip!

Of course, there's a lot more you can do when traveling alone, but these are a few tips and places to start. There are also experiences that are geared toward single people and some packages that are best suited for solo travelers. Just take the appropriate precautions and choose your lodging wisely. Once you don't have to worry about safety, you're free to enjoy the rest of your trip to the fullest!

With a little research, you'll be just fine traveling anywhere. Need a little more help? Check out the Extras for some resources and additional advice! There are safety and packing tips, travel journal ideas, and resources for planning and preparing for your next getaway.

Chapter 16: Social Night

In the last few chapters, we've really focused on activities you can do alone, but here's the thing: when you're single, you shouldn't spend all your free time alone. Like we talked about in the beginning of the book, you should aim for a balance between socialization and alone time that's right for you. So when you're looking to be social, look to those around you for a good time. Organize a night out with your friends. If you're close to your family, get together for a game night. The possibilities are endless! And the great thing about friends and family is that you can often take them places and do activities with them that you may have done with a significant other, and it won't make anything as weird and awkward as if you had gone alone.

You can do most, if not all, of the activities we talked about in this book with friends, and some might even be more enjoyable if you have someone along for the ride. You can also include a friend in a lot of the activities listed in the Extras if you want to! There's nothing that says you can't as long as it's fun for you. Friends are also great for getting you into new things and going on adventures with you, so you can all experience something new.

Having regular social interactions with people who know you is important to helping you grow as a person. We are all affected by those around us and because you're single, you'll want to be even more mindful of how many different perspectives there are in your life. Having a partner typically comes with a built-in person to give you a little reality check when you're getting stuck in your ways. If you're regularly socializing with friends and family who think differently from you and you all enjoy broadening your horizons, that's even better!

Socializing with new people is also a great way to make sure you're still exercising your social muscles. Meeting new people in a no-pressure, non-relationship-centric environment is a really fun way to spend an evening or a weekend. Often times, you'll just run into people as you're going about an activity you fully planned on doing alone, and you'll make a few new acquaintances along the way that share your interest. Having someone to chat with, even just for the duration of the activity, makes something like a class or a sport that much more enjoyable. You also might learn a thing or two!

The Internet is also a great way to meet new friends and maintain friendships across long distances and with busy schedules. Social media comes with its drawbacks, of course, which we've covered in the past chapters, but it's often worth it when you have the intention of finding a group of people to call your friends. There are countless groups on social media, Discord servers, chat rooms, and other forums where you can meet and interact with people from all over the world that share your same interests.

Having a group of people, whether they all know each other or not, to share your journey with will help you make the most of your situation. Humans take comfort in the knowledge that our trials have some meaning, and what better meaning is there than being able to help those around you through your experiences? Social gatherings are a good opportunity to come together with people you trust to share your experiences and learn with and from each other. You can share everything you've learned from this book and from your own experiences with those around you to get not only their insight into how you could improve your life, but to also be able to enrich their lives and help them or someone they know who may be struggling as well. This attitude toward socialization, along with the desire to have a good time and bond with others, is what really keeps us going, no matter what our relationship status is. Social nights can be more than just fun and games, and that's good too. Like everything else we've talked about in this book, achieving balance is of the utmost importance.

If you like a degree of anonymity when sharing about your personal life, there are many online groups and forums where you can build a community of people to share some aspects of your life with. Sometimes having the protection of the online community helps us be more open and honest because we're all naturally braver behind computer screens. And in this case, that's totally okay. Of course, we all know that the Internet is not without its problems, so take everything you do online with a grain of salt and a bit of caution; but that's the world in which we live, and we're all somewhat used to it by now.

While we're on the topic of words of caution, be careful of singles groups. They'll come up in a later chapter where we get into deciding whether you'd like to be single long term, but here's a sneak peek:

> Because let's face it, most "singles" groups definitely have that vibe of "we're all looking for someone and this is just a dating pool to choose from." That's probably not the most comfortable environment for you if you're not thinking about dating for a while. We talked about this before as well, but who you surround yourself with really does have an impact on your overall happiness. At the end of the day, you are in control of your happiness, but make sure that you're not surrounding yourself with people that are pressuring you to live a way you don't want to.

Singles groups have taken on this role in society that is reinforcing the concept that you need someone to be happy. If you're just looking to hang out with other single people, you'd think this is a logical step, right? That sure would be nice! Pardon the sarcastic attitude, but it's a little tough to figure out where to find your community. Of course, you can always give a group or two a try—not all of them are going to be the same—but that potential issue is definitely worth mentioning (a few times).

As advertised in previous chapters, you may find your community during a class or activity. Those types of more socially engaging activities definitely count as social time and may even help you find a group of long-term friends. Don't worry—the Internet is definitely not your only hope to find a group of like-minded people to hang out with.

Of course, there are a few folks out there who aren't looking for long-term friendships either. It's common to be burnt out on relationships of all kinds when you're taking a step back from dating after a bad experience. There's nothing wrong with wanting or needing to take a break, no matter what society may tell you. This chapter was really long-term friendship heavy, and it's important to highlight that that's not the only valid way to have a fulfilling social life. If you're just looking for a low-pressure passing thing, the Internet (yes, that again!) is a great way to socialize without the stress of having to maintain any kind of relationship with anyone. It's worth noting that this kind of social behavior is not a sustainable practice, and if you find that this is how you're operating for more than a year, it might be worth considering if there's an area of growth that may need your attention.

Socializing is like exercising: continuing to do so and to try to build and maintain relationships is healthy, and your skills and confidence will improve like muscle definition and stamina does when you exercise. That may be a strange analogy, but for all you fitness enthusiasts out there, you know what it means. So, however you choose to do it, make sure you're at least trying to spend some time with other people on a semi-regular schedule. Even if you're an introvert, you will start to feel some serious adverse effects if you step out of the social world for too long.

Like anything that's worth doing, building and maintaining your friendships takes time and effort. When you're trying to figure out your new life as a single person, consider the balance between alone and social time in your schedule (yes, yes, you've heard it before—it's worth mentioning again, though!). Consider the following cautions from the chapter on energy:

Hopefully you've never experienced total burnout before, but if you're familiar with it, burnout happens at a lot of jobs when you're overworked and stressed constantly where you can't enjoy a work/life balance. Burnout doesn't just come from jobs, though. In fact, it may have been burnout that caused you to give up the search for a romantic partner and start reading this book. You can get burned out on any activity you do frequently without an adequate break.

Emotional energy is hard to quantify, even though we've all felt when we run low on it at some point in our lives. We expend emotional energy when we listen to someone else's problems, try to offer council, or do something that is emotionally difficult like having a hard conversation with someone. Feeling intense emotions also takes or generates emotional energy. Positive emotions typically leave you with more emotional energy than you had before, where negative emotions leave you feeling drained.

When you're running low on emotional energy, it's hard to deal with stress. Oddly enough, it's easy to respond more strongly to things when you're drained emotionally, even though those responses take more energy. It's a hard cycle to break. This cycle also contributes to burnout and difficulty in relationships.

The good news is that emotional energy does come back pretty easily. To regain emotional energy, all you typically have to do is take a break from emotionally intense activities and interactions. Staying away from drama is helpful in regaining emotional energy, as is not consuming news for a little while.

These notes, while having been drilled into you across this book, are absolutely tied to socialization and a lack of balance. Consider burnout and balance in your life, as well as how your emotional energy levels may be warning you of toxic relationships. Yes, toxicity isn't just limited to dating relationships. Believe it or not, friendships can be toxic and harmful too. Hopefully you don't know what that's like firsthand and you never will, but it's something to watch out for. It's a two-way street, too. If you're running low on emotional energy, you might end up being the one who's doing more harm than good. That's not meant to scare you, just to help you keep in mind the balance that will help you truly enjoy your social nights and be the friend that you wish to see in the world.

No matter how you choose to spend your social time, being intentional about that time is important. That's why there's an emphasis on planning or organizing time with friends and family, so that you're all setting aside dedicated time to build your relationships and have fun together. We set aside time for what's important to us. Social time is one of those things that's essential to our growth and happiness as people.

Part IV: Where Does Your Journey End?

Well, reader, we've come to that point in our discussion on being single where we should probably address what kind of lifestyle you're settling into and for how long you'd like to be single. It's a really hard question to answer, and even if you think you know what your answer will be, life has a way of surprising us all. So, here's the thing: the amount of time and energy you invest into building a life as a single person that you can be happy and comfortable in has everything to do with how you view your journey. If you think you'll be single "forever" (the foreseeable future), you're probably going to take the advice in Part III to heart a lot quicker than someone who just wants to get by for a few months while they figure themselves out and then plans to get back out there.

What are your thoughts? How do you view your dating life (or lack thereof)? Do you think you'd like to be single long term? How do you figure out the answer? Then, how do you come to terms with it? This part of the book will help shed some light on the self-actualization process involved in making those kinds of decisions and how to go from there. We'll review some points we covered in the first few chapters to see what changes about the decision-making elements and what else we can learn from those chapters now that we're thinking about being single in a different way.

As you're reading, please keep in mind that everything is a choice and can be changed later. While our actions and mindset do affect how we interact with the outside world, this part of your journey is very personal, and you don't have to try to fit this mold if you don't want to. If for nothing else, let these next few chapters be food for thought. Who knows— you might learn something unexpected about yourself along the way!

Chapter 17: Lifestyle or Circumstance? How to Figure Out If You Want to Be Single Long Term

By now, you've gotten a pretty good idea of everything singles' life has to offer. Sounds good, doesn't it? Hopefully you've found comfort and peace in your decision to remain single for a while and you have more ideas of what you can do with your free time than you actually have time for! There are certainly worse problems to have!

If you've been single for a long time by the time you're reading this, you may have already started thinking about when, if ever, you'd like to start dating again. Maybe you're newly single and the earlier chapters in Part I got you thinking.

We phrased everything in Part I in terms of "yet," "right now," and other such qualifiers that would indicate to others that you're not committed to being single and would be open to starting to date later on. We even encouraged you to do the same when you're talking to yourself or anyone else. But just because you say those things to other people, doesn't mean it has to be true. You may say, "I'm not looking for a relationship right now," to your co-worker who keeps trying to set you up with someone from their book group, but when you're thinking about your journey as a single person, do you really feel like "right now" is true?

If your immediate answer was "no," don't be alarmed! In a lot of ways, that means you've learned everything we could ever teach you about being comfortable and happy as a single person—so much so that you now truly enjoy being single! Good for you! That also means that you might benefit from going back and rereading Part I through your new lens of settling into this lifestyle permanently. Just skip over those parts about how to soften your verbiage for other people.

So, how do you even know when it's time to make your decision to be single long term or to go back into the dating pool? It's a lot easier to know when it's the right time to start dating again because either someone will cross your path that you're interested in being in a relationship with and you'll want to go for it, or you'll feel ready to start dating again because no matter how happy and comfortable you were alone, you feel like something was missing and you're ready for your next adventure.

To know that you want to remain single is a little bit more complicated. Unless you had already made up your mind back when we were talking about knowing when to stop looking for a partner, you've got a little soul-searching ahead of you. There's a lot that goes into making that decision because being in a relationship really does affect every part of your life.

Start by imagining your future. What do you see? That right there might tell you if there's some point in your life where you should try dating again. If you don't see yourself with a partner, then start thinking about your career goals and your life goals. Somewhere in there, ask yourself why you think you want to still be single. Ask yourself what you'll gain or lose if you have a partner. The answer to the bigger question of whether you should settle into singles' life long term will come to you.

And remember, even if you say you're going to be single permanently, there's nothing holding you to that. Maybe in a few decades someone will cross your path and you'll be ready to pursue a life with them. It helps to consider your decision to be single for the foreseeable future as an indefinite singleness rather than a permanent state. However you want to think about your relationship status to help yourself become more comfortable with it is totally up to you. Just remember that it's all a choice, and you'll feel a lot more comfortable once you own that decision and know you're going to make the most of it.

So why is it so important to make this delineation between being single until you find someone and choosing to be single indefinitely without any plans to start looking for someone? How you think about the single lifestyle regarding your long-term relationship goals will affect how you begin your journey more than you'd imagine.

At the beginning of our journey together, we talked about how to know when to stop looking for a partner. But we had that conversation forever ago, so let's take a little trip down memory lane.

It's understandable if you feel conflicted about whether to give up the search for your perfect partner. Whether you've been burned by the process before or you've never found the right person, it's a big decision to call off the search.

So, how do you know when to stop looking for a relationship? There's really no one-size-fits-all answer to that question. To find out for yourself what's right for you, take a look at your schedule for a week and see how much time you're devoting to searching for a partner. Then compare it to everything else you've got to take care of every day. Are you falling behind on things? Are there tasks you wish you could accomplish that have to fall by the wayside because you're spending all your free time looking for a partner? That could be a sign that you should call off the search for a little while. Of course, that shouldn't be the only factor upon which you base your decision, but it's a red flag if you've been neglecting things you want to or have to do in favor of looking for a partner. Moderation in how you spend your time is key in maintaining happiness and your ability to handle stresses like looking for a partner. If how you use your time is out of balance, it's probably worth taking a break from looking for a relationship to work on yourself so you find the search less taxing when you pick it back up again.

Another red flag that's probably telling you to stop looking for a relationship is your success rate. If you're having a hard time finding someone or you keep having bad experiences dating, it's probably time to take a break for a little while. Now, your dating success rate is affected by a lot of circumstances that are not under your control, but there are some key factors that you can actually control. Things like where you're meeting potential partners, the dating pool, and what you're looking for in a partner and relationship can all contribute to an excellent or terrible success rate when it comes to dating.

To help you feel better, none of the following paragraph is in any way blaming anyone. We all strike out sometimes—

that's totally okay and no reason to feel bad about yourself. It's just helpful to know what might be causing looking for a relationship to be more trouble than it's worth.

If you feel like you're doing everything right and your search is still not turning up any romantic matches, that's okay. It's discouraging, but certainly not uncommon or something to be ashamed of. One of the worst things you can do for yourself long term is settle for someone just because you don't want to be alone. Keep your standards and wait until the right person comes along. Sometimes that right person will cross your path when you least expect it. Have faith in that, try taking a break from actively looking for a partner, and see if someone comes along in your daily life.

Now that you've dedicated some time to exploring why you might not have found someone even though you're investing a lot of time and effort into looking, let's talk about how you might be feeling about your search and about the prospect of choosing to stop the search for now. For some people, it's easy to make the decision. In fact, your mind may have already been made up before you even started reading. Having your mind made up can come with some nerves, though, because society has spent so long telling us that we need a romantic relationship in order to be happy and heavily implies that there's something wrong with us when we're single. It's okay to wonder "what if the right person comes along the day after I delete the dating app?" Or, "what if I never find someone?" But here's the thing: if that person was "right" for you, they would have been put in your path while you were still on the dating site. The right person will always be in front of you at the right time in both of your lives. We'll talk more about that in a later chapter, but it's worth mentioning now. As far as not finding someone, "never" is a strong word. Just because you've stopped looking for now, doesn't mean that you won't start looking again somewhere down the line or that you won't meet someone organically as you're going about your daily life. Trust your gut: if you feel as though you should stop looking for a relationship, don't let your culture make you feel nervous or guilty for the choice that's right for you.

So, you've made the choice to be single and put down the dating app. What now? How do you tell people (if you have to) that you're not looking for anyone right now? How do you justify it in your own mind? The next two chapters are your first steps to ensuring your comfort as a single person.

Before we move on, it's worth highlighting that being single is a choice, and you have to own it for any of this advice to work for you. Owning the choice to be single doesn't mean you have to brag about it, or that you have to make yourself be confident in it automatically. Owning your decision is all about understanding that you do have control over your relationships and whether you stay in the dating game and when, if ever, you get back into it. As you progress through this book, you'll build confidence in your decision and that confidence will directly translate to how comfortable you are as a single person. It all starts with answering a key question for yourself.

Chapter 1 really did set us up for success in understanding what goes into the process of figuring out if you want to be single in the first place. All of those tips and tricks are also super helpful in making the jump to being single more permanently. Ultimately, making that decision is really just making the decision to be single all over again.

The good news, dear reader, is you have some experience in this arena already! Congrats on the leg up! It's still good to have a reminder of the process, though, since it may have been some time since you decided to stop the search for a partner.

Another great piece of advice is to imagine what your life will look like in a year, five years, and so on to see if there's a future you can see in which you would want a partner. Whatever you think your future will hold at this moment should show you what you want down the line. And just because you may want a partner in a decade or whenever you see it coming up in your grand plan doesn't mean you have to give up on the idea that you want to be single for an extended period of time *now*. It's just some food for thought.

When you're imagining your future, be mindful of some warning signs that you're not setting yourself up for success:

1. Does your future include other people like family or friends?
2. When you imagine a day in your life five years from now, are you all alone?
3. How do you feel when you're imagining your future?
4. Can you even conceive of a decade from now?
5. Do you have things you're looking forward to?

Having those questions in mind when you try to imagine your future and whether you think you might want someone romantically in it later on will really help give you some clarity on more arenas than just your love life. If you don't feel happy and excited about your future, there might be something you should look into to turn that frown upside down. It's hard to get excited about things that may never be, but having a goal of how you want your life to look and being able to work toward something you're excited about is part of a healthy lifestyle. That extends far outside of the realm of finding happiness as a single person, but it really does bear mentioning.

After reading all of this, how are you feeling about the decision to be single long term? If you've still got some reservations, it might be worth putting off the decision for a while longer. It's not like anyone needs you to make that decision immediately.

If it makes you nervous to commit to removing the "yet" and "for now" from your mindset regarding your single life, don't do it. This type of decision is only for your own use and no one else has to know whether you've decided to be single long term or are just waiting until you feel ready to get back out there. As we mentioned earlier, making the decision helps you be more intentional in your habit formation and allows you to prepare for the feelings and questions that may come up over your career as a single person. Speaking of which, Chapter 3 had a lot to say about preparing to answer certain questions and responding to assumptions about your singleness. Let's take a look at how that chapter can help us at this new stage of your life.

Chapter 18: Chapter 3, but Imagined Differently

Here's the new version of Chapter 3 for those who don't want to date again. There's not a major difference, but it's worth repeating with a few modifications.

One of the great things about being single for a while is that you become a pro at answering questions about being single. However, there are a whole host of questions that come up after no one hears about you going out on a date for a while, or, once you reach a certain age in some cultures, why you're not married. But like we covered back in Chapter 3, once you're confident in your own motivations for staying single, the answers will come easily. The first few may blindside you, but you'll be a pro in no time.

To help with that, think back on a few of the points from Chapter 3. Since it's been so long since we've talked about any of it, and going all the way back to the beginning of the book is just awkward, let's look at some of the points we went over earlier and see what, if anything, changes about how to approach peoples' questions now that you're planning to be single long term.

Something to keep in mind as you're reading (and a very important reminder from Chapter 3)*: Don't be defensive. Being casual and open about being single goes a long way in stopping probing questions or lines of discussion that you'd rather not participate* *in, and it comes from a place of self-assurance and comfort.* Like when you're new to being single, it's a process to build up your confidence. If you're at the point where you're considering being single long term, even if you felt confident being single and fielding those questions with the qualifiers of "right now," you may feel a little less confident now that you know that "right now" may be more of a stretch than anyone knows.

Another thing to think about is the assumptions that people are making about you. We talked about this regarding asking why you're single. Here's what Chapter 3 has to say about assumptions: *The assumption that you need to be in a relationship in order to be happy is what typically drives people to ask those kinds of questions.* This means questions about your relationship status. It is still absolutely true. Even though it can be tiring over the months or years of fielding those questions, it's important to remember that ordinarily, they are coming from a good place (or at the very least a place of blissful unawareness), and it helps to keep that in mind so you're not defensive when the subject comes up. Knowing that you don't have to agree with those assumptions also helps you hold firm to your decision to be happy as a single person.

Yes, even if they tack on "still" to any of those probing questions, they probably mean well and just don't quite land the question how they wanted to. Hearing someone ask, "how are you still single?" both sarcastically and literally is a common thing. If you know that the person is asking you literally, they probably mean well and are trying to say that you're a person that they think would make a great partner. The good thing about that type of question's phrasing is that you can treat it almost like a rhetorical question and just shrug. Odds are, they don't actually want to know the details of how you're still single. But then, that's just an assumption...

It's really hard not to get defensive the tenth time someone asks you why you're still single. So, how do you avoid getting a little snippy with that aunt or sibling that makes a comment at a family gathering for the thousandth time? (Because let's be honest, it's always the family members that notice first, right?)

One of the best things you can do is to not answer right away. No one's saying you have to take a dramatic pause, but the first few seconds are crucial. If you say the first thing that pops into your head and you're already feeling a little frustrated that you even have to answer that question, whatever you say next will probably come out differently than you intend it to. Take even an extra second to think about what you were about to say and if it's really what you wanted to say and how you wanted to say it. As a bonus, having that somewhat awkward pause might help dissuade that particular person from asking you again, because it wasn't a super pleasant conversation the first time. You may be concerned that having a few seconds' pause before you answer will make it look like they caught you off guard, but that's honestly the last thing you need to be worried about, especially if you want to preserve the relationship with whomever you're talking with. Being slow to speak and slower to anger is a good thing to learn and internalize for a wide variety of interactions.

Something we didn't really touch on in Chapter 3 that truly does bear mentioning in this section is not overexplaining. Nervous talking is a problem for some people, and others just feel like they have to explain everything in detail so that others fully understand where they're coming from (okay, that's a little bit like this book is in some places, but not quite the same!). The fastest way to beat that habit - and this may sound harsh - is to remind yourself that no one cares that much. Of course, that's not always the case and those close to you may really be interested in how you arrived at the decision to be single indefinitely, but co-workers and other people you're not as close to genuinely probably don't want a twenty minute explanation of how you came to that conclusion.

To help yourself feel less nervous when the conversation veers over into relationships, either dodge the question if you can do so without making it look like you're dodging or to have a general, short, and vague answer ready that works for a variety of situations. Feeling prepared helps you stay away from nervous chatter that you'll regret later. If you're able to redirect the question, asking another question or showing interest in another topic adjacent to the current topic is helpful, and it makes you appear more personable. Most folks like to talk rather than listen, so if you ask them a question, it's likely they'll be answering long before they realize you didn't answer their question. You can also employ a combination of the two methods (this is often the most effective) and give a short answer and then redirect the conversation to avoid any follow up questions and to stop yourself from nervous chatter. (Does this sound like advice for interviewing? Maybe a little. It's also good to remember in professional conversations too—just a little side note.)

So, what do those short and polite answers sound like? If you're blessed with a good sense of humor, you can go with something witty like, "I'm just having a good time," or something similar that serves as a one-size-fits-most type of response to a wide variety of comments and questions. Notice there's no mention of your relationship status and it's a non-controversial statement. You would be hard pressed to find someone who wants to argue with a statement like that and it really shuts down that line of conversation—so now you have the opening to ask someone else a question or otherwise redirect the conversation however you want to take the heat off yourself. If you don't feel like trying to be funny, you can always make an "I" statement like "I like being single." It's far more direct and to the point, but if said kindly it won't come off as hostile. It could leave you open to someone asking you why, and that's not a bad thing if it's the right time and place for you to explain your process to them. Who knows, maybe you're helping them with their own process!

Another note made in Chapter 3 is about peoples' reaction to your life choices: *It's such a strange thing that people feel as though their choice to be in a relationship is in any way tied to your choice to be single, but a lot of people do, and more direct answers can cause them to feel offended. Responding in a neutral way shows that you're not closed off to the idea of finding someone or putting yourself out there, but you just don't want to right now. And, assuming that you know the person you're talking with well, they will be happy that you're happy and will likely leave the topic alone because they just want what's best for you.* While this was written alongside the notes to include "right now," or similar, at the end of your answers, it still rings true now that you're probably going to drop those qualifiers. Understanding where people are coming from and how quickly they could get offended, no matter how diplomatic you are, is very important. It's not your fault that some people choose to take offense from you choosing to be single when they're in a relationship or still looking for someone. Odds are, they're struggling to be comfortable and secure in their own decision, and their response actually has little to do with you and your choices. Hopefully that helps you survive those types of interactions.

Speaking of surviving interactions, let's talk more about those family members who are interested in your relationship status. We touched on them briefly earlier in this chapter, but Chapter 3 had some interesting things to say as well:

> *But from the people that know you best, there can come more dangerous comments. Comments like, "you're too picky," and questions like, "why can't you just find someone?" can really be hurtful, especially coming from someone like a parent or a close family member. The good news is, since you're likely very close with the person saying these things, you can be more direct and honest. It's usually more acceptable for you to say something like, "It's not that I'm picky, I just want to spend some time focusing on myself right now." The better you know the person, the more specific your answers can typically be. The truth will set you free. But remember, try not to be defensive. A calm answer comes from a place of comfort and happiness in your singleness, and how you respond conveys that to the people you're interacting with. If they pick up on how comfortable you are with being single and with getting those comments, they will likely accept your answers much more readily than if you seem taken aback or defensive.*

We can also add in fun little comments to the effect of "what's wrong with you that you can't find a partner?" Assumptions that there's something wrong with you for being single for the past few years can be incredibly hurtful. No one's encouraging you to let those comments roll off your back. If you're able to tell the person who made that comment that it hurt you, you absolutely should. But you're not always able to, and that's the hard part. As much as this book preaches confidence, comfort, and security in your decision to be single, no matter for how long, there's no goal to strive for or standard you have to meet all the time. You shouldn't feel bad about yourself for feeling hurt or stressed out by these comments and questions. We're all humans—we feel things, and we don't always react how we wish we would have. It's life, and it's okay.

This book is just a guide for a few ideas of how to respond in these types of situations. The point of this little bunny trail was to show that you can respond to family members a little differently *because* they're family. There's also a higher chance of family members commenting on your relationship than nearly anyone else in your life because they've probably known you the longest and feel comfortable enough to ask some pretty intense questions. It also means that you might have a fair shot at actually explaining your journey and thought process to them because they'll probably listen a lot more than anyone else. Family is complicated, but they're likely just coming from a place of concern for you that's influenced by a relationship-centric society that has them worried you're not going to be happy when you're single.

Speaking of a relationship-centric society, what about the media? You know, that fun thing that colors how we get our information and how we see the world these days? The advice in Chapter 3 was great for being single for a little while, especially in that adjustment period at the beginning where you're still solidifying yourself as a single person, but there are a few key things in here that might need to be adjusted over time:

> *The reality is, if we tried to cut all relationship-centric media out of our lives, we wouldn't have much media left to consume. And that's not the answer, anyway! Relationships make for excellent comedic relief and help lots of plot points, but the trick is to find media that doesn't send the message that you'll only be happy when you're in a relationship. Only you know what kind of media is good for your mental health, so just keep this in mind when you're looking for a movie to watch on a Saturday night; and if you're already feeling a little down, maybe don't turn on that rom-com and find a good old-fashioned comedy instead.*

Of course, it's a great idea at the beginning to get away from relationship-centric media to help yourself not feel sad or like you're missing out on something because you're not seeing someone. However, we talked about sustainable habits as a long-term single person, and this is not one of them. Maybe you can find a niche of media out there that has nothing to do with relationships and doesn't have a pro-relationship agenda, and if so, you're incredibly lucky (and also, what did you search? Please share with the rest of us!). But odds are, relationship-centric media will be a part of your life. The good news is as you're more confident and comfortable as a single person and strong in your decision to be single, so media really won't have an effect on you anymore.

Having good boundaries between what's funny to see on the TV screen and what applies to your own life is extremely important to ensure your happiness. Of course rom-coms are going have an agenda that doesn't necessarily align with your own. But as in real-life conversations, the choices of those in the media don't have to match your own, and you can just enjoy the media without having to buy into the agenda or the messages that media sends. That was just a little nuanced for Chapter 3. That adjustment period is a different ballgame, as you probably know by now. Now that you're farther along in your journey as a single person, odds are you're more than able to shut off your doubts and just enjoy media for what it is.

Before we move on, here's a last bit of advice from Chapter 3 that sums up most of what we've been talking about and a good tip on how to avoid any questions about your relationship status:

When people ask you about your relationship status, keep your tone light and casual and just tell them you're not looking for a relationship. If you make it sound like no big deal, they likely won't make it one. It's honestly not most people's business if you're looking for someone or not, and they won't push the subject. It'll feel awkward at first, and you might feel like you have to explain, but you really don't. It also helps to avoid phrasing things in ways that will highlight that you're single. You can always say "we" when you're talking about doing things with other people instead of specifying who you were with, and that wording will often lead people to believe that you did whatever activity with your romantic partner rather than your best friend. It might feel like you have to hide that you're single, and that really doesn't help with the confidence part of figuring out how to be single, but knowing why you're choosing to phrase your response those ways does help you to become more confident. We don't always tell everyone everything and choose not to open ourselves up to judgement by others. It's one thing to feel bad about being single within your own mind, but it's somehow worse when you're opened up to someone else judging you. The first step is to own your decision, and the wording will come easily after that.

At the end of the day, your relationship status is no one's business but your own. In Chapter 1, we talked about how to come to terms with being single and relearning how to look at your singleness. Keep both Chapter 1 and this chapter bookmarked, or write down any key takeaways from both chapters and look at them often. Everything in this book is about a process that's uniquely personal and is meant to be customized to your own journey and mental health. There are so many ways of dealing with these questions and stumbling blocks, and you'll have some ideas of your own as you go through these situations on your own.

Hopefully that helped you a little bit. You can also always continue to add the "right now's" and "at the moment's" if it makes you feel more comfortable. That's the point, isn't it? You have to be comfortable—it matters more how you feel than anyone else. Just make sure that whatever you choose to say to people will reinforce what you tell yourself. That way, you will be the most confident in your decision that you can be.

Chapter 19: Being Indefinitely Single: What They Don't Tell You

So, what don't they tell you about being single indefinitely? Well, in most cases, no one tells us anything in popular media. You really have to go looking for those types of answers, and then you still have to check the bias to make sure the resources you've found aren't pushing you toward getting into a relationship even though you don't want to. When you're looking for advice, books like this one are your best bet for guidance on how to settle in long term, unless you know someone who happens to have some experience in that arena.

If you haven't noticed by now, this book is all about helping you be the happiest and most comfortable you can be as a single person. If you're planning on being single for the foreseeable future, there's not a lot out there that prepares you for that lifestyle. Most cultures don't really talk about what you have to look forward to when you don't want to be in a relationship. That goes back to what we talked about in the beginning chapters regarding what society tells us in the media about being in relationships in order to be happy and fulfilled. That's why having this little section is so important to reference.

A lot of the tips and tricks are pretty much the same whether you're planning on being single long term or just for a little while. So, the middle sections of this book are just as useful to you as they are to someone who wants to just take a breather before they get back into the dating game. All that really changes is your mindset and your level of dedication in forming a routine and a set of sustainable habits that help you make the most of being single.

You've probably seen this in a million different places, but forming habits is important as an adult. It's made even easier in a lot of ways by being single because you have more freedom to experiment with what habits work for you, and you don't have to try to work around someone else's (unless you have a roommate, that is). If you can, try to start forming a routine including any of the tips from the past chapters that work for you. Having a routine will help you form habits that you can take with you for the rest of your life. Having a routine also allows you to be more present in your everyday life and enjoy the most you can.

Another thing not a lot of people tell you about being single indefinitely is that there are other people out there just like you. So when you're thinking about building your community and you know you want to be single for a while, it's nice to surround yourself with people who are like-minded and won't put pressure on you to find someone. Because let's face it, most "singles" groups are just groups of people looking for who to date next. That's probably not the most comfortable environment for you if you're not thinking about dating for a while. We talked about this before as well, but who you surround yourself with really does have an impact on your overall happiness. At the end of the day, you are in control of your happiness, but make sure that you're not surrounding yourself with people that are pressuring you to live a way you don't want to.

That's not to say that if you went on Discord and searched for a server with the search words "long-term singles" that you'd find something, but as you're building your community around other interests, activities, or whatever may be bringing you together, you'll find people more like you who want to be single for a while. If you're looking, your community will find you.

One thing to consider (or confront) is that nagging feeling of wondering if there's something wrong with you that causes you to want to be single indefinitely. Of course, we've touched on how to answer the big question of why you want to be single a few times by now, but what no one really tells you is how to kick that feeling that there's something secretly wrong with you for *not* wanting to be in a relationship. No matter how you may answer the big question, it doesn't ensure that you're not silently freaking out about if there's something wrong with you. (If that doesn't ring a bell for you, you're one of the lucky ones!)

But if you read that paragraph and felt like this book just saw into your soul, first off, apologies! Secondly, you're not alone. You just wouldn't know it because no one wants to show you that there's a way to kick that feeling without throwing yourself into a relationship or getting some drastic makeover and then getting into a relationship. (Yes, this was a dig at pop culture and the media's representation of single people. We're on the same page about the media by now, right?) The media sure does show us that there's something wrong with those who want to be single long term an awful lot, but any type of meaningful solution to that question has yet to become popular. This is yet another exercise in not listening to the subtext in popular media for the sake of your comfort and happiness as a single person. Here's what the media doesn't tell you: If you're wondering what's wrong with you, ask yourself the same questions you asked yourself at the beginning of this process, as well as a few more in-depth follow-up questions:

- Why don't I want to be in a relationship?
- Did something happen to cause me to want to make being single a lifestyle instead of a temporary thing?
  - If yes, that's probably as far as you need to go. You have a good reason for why you're not interested in being in a relationship and that's okay. The feeling that something's wrong with you will fade away. If it comes back, just remind yourself of why (in non-traumatizing and somewhat general terms so you don't dredge up bad memories) and you'll feel better.
  - If no, that's a good thing! You don't need trauma or bad experiences to justify your choice. Odds are, though, that you're going to be the one that's most worried about figuring out what's wrong with you for not wanting to be in a relationship. Hang in there!

If your answers to those two questions were not enlightening and you're truly worried that there's something wrong, consider seeking professional help. "They" (the media and pop culture) definitely show therapy a lot more these days, but it's rare that anyone makes the connection that you can ask a therapist or licensed counselor if they can offer any additional insight.

If seeking professional help isn't possible for you or just isn't your cup of tea, maybe this book can be of a little more help to you. It's helpful to explore what may be "wrong" with you first to eliminate that as an option so you can arrive at the knowledge that there isn't anything wrong with you for wanting to be single.

Let's also come away from using "wrong" now that we're having a deeper discussion about this topic. That's the first thing you can do to help yourself—reserve self-judgement until you've considered all the facts and possibilities. So, here we go. Consider your attitude toward humanity and socializing with others. If Chapter 16 was an absolute pain for you to get through or you find that you give up on people too easily, that may actually be a sign of a deeper problem. To resolve this, take a look at your mental and emotional energy levels and consider this advice from Chapter 6:

By identifying the energy drains in your life, you can assess whether you can make any changes to prevent deeper issues from arising as a result of being out of energy for a long time.

Some common emotional energy drains are:
- *Trying to find a romantic partner*
- *Toxic relationships, platonic or otherwise*
- *Drama, whether you're in it or just watching*
- *High-emotion situations*
- *Emotional whiplash*
- *Anxiety and other mental illnesses*

That's quite the list, isn't it? And there may even be long-term stresses in your life that aren't on this list. Everyone has stress. It's not good for us, but it is a part of life and we can't expect to completely eradicate it from our world. The good news is that we can still be happy and comfortable in our lives even when we're stressed. The key to developing good coping mechanisms is to identify the big stresses in your life before you feel overwhelmed.

You'll know better than anyone what works for you. Go with your gut as long as it's not going to harm you in the long run. So, don't eat as a way of reducing stress, get blackout drunk every night, or anything else that might harm you. That's not what we're going for with this. What we're aiming for are healthy, sustainable strategies for regaining your energy. Most stresses in life are long term, so do your best to develop habits and practices that are just as sustainable so you have ways to increase your energy every day.

The umbrella advice for regaining energy is reducing your stress, both internal and external. Mental stress can be controlled more easily than stress coming at you from things outside your mind (and potentially your control). So, focus on how to reduce your stress daily. This could be a self-care routine, watching a TV show that makes you laugh, calling a friend or family member, working out, or meditating. You have so many options to reduce stress that there's bound to be at least one out there that will work for you!

You'll find when you're managing your stress and energy levels, even if nothing about your life or social situations have changed yet, you'll still feel so much more comfortable and in control of your life.

Those words of advice on mitigating your burnout and regaining your energy may help you either feel a sense of relief that you're doing everything you can to not let burnout be the cause of you wanting to be single indefinitely, or show that there's something you can do to solve the underlying problems that are causing you to feel as though something's wrong.

Another thing they don't tell you is that you can try getting back into the dating arena for a night or two to make sure you remember what it's like and that you truly are just not interested in doing it for a while. This is the closest to what the media shows us, but it typically ends in a happily ever after of some sort when it's on the silver screen. What they don't tell you is that it's totally okay to come back from a speed dating or match-making event and just go, "Okay, I didn't have a good time. I don't want to do that again." It's reality, and the media just doesn't want to show you that you do have an out. By confirming that you're just not crazy about it, you'll probably find some peace in your decision.

No matter how you approach being single indefinitely, there's a lot that no one tells you. Like many things in life, we just have to figure it out for ourselves. Hopefully there was something in all of that information that will help you become better informed and more confident in your decision to be single for the foreseeable future. Before you move on, or in case you need to hear this: you are valid, you are worthy of happiness, and you will find comfort and happiness in the lifestyle that is right for you.

Part V: At the End of the Road...

We've gone over pretty much everything you may be worried about when it comes to being single, knowing when to stop the search for a partner, and how to make the most of your time as a single person. We've also briefly mentioned being ready to start looking for that special someone again. Of course, if your life plan has always involved being in a relationship, it's probably a relief to you that you're going to settle down again at some point. Either way, it's important to welcome the next stage of your life without regrets. That means living your life as a single person so you don't have any of them.

The best suggestion to make sure you're not going to regret any part of the single stage of your life is to take a look at how you're spending your time and who you're spending it with. Just ask yourself every now and then, "Am I going to have regrets? Is there something I'm not doing or doing that I wish I would (or wouldn't)?" Even once you're back in a relationship, checking in is a good habit to have for the rest of your life to help avoid regrets.

To make sure you don't have any regrets in the present about how you're living your life as a single person, try making a bucket list for your time as one. It's a weird idea, but it's not only a fun exercise—it's also a productive one. Take a look at some of the activities in the Extras section, think about things you've always wanted to do but no one's wanted to do with you or you haven't had the time yet, and make a list. Keep it somewhere where you'll be able to reference it and try to cross a few things off the list before you get back into a relationship. And if you don't get them all done, maybe there are some that you can actually do with your partner or alone even though you're dating! It's not like the bucket list is a list of tasks to be accomplished before you're "allowed" to get back into a relationship. The point is to have fun with it and get whatever is on there crossed off if you have the opportunity to.

Making these bucket lists is also a fun group activity. If you've found your community of like-minded individuals, maybe making the bucket list is a great wine-night activity to do with friends to get a good laugh and some interesting ideas. There's no reason to take this or yourself as a single person too seriously. Enjoy the process and keep adding to the list as you see things that you think sound like a good time! Having a good bucket list is a great way to avoid regrets before they get the chance to upset the next stage of your life.

All this talk about regrets isn't meant to get you down, though! The goal is to make sure that you're as happy as you can be during this new part of your life. Being single, like anything else in life, serves a purpose. There's probably something you're going to take with you from that part of your life that you'll carry with you forever and pass along to other people who are where you are now. Even though you're reading this now when you're still single, bookmark this part for when you're ready to get back into a relationship.

Also remember, no matter the title of this part of the book, the end of your career as a single person isn't the end of your road by any means. Your free time might look a little different once you start dating (but you probably already know that). However, there are so many resources out there for how to keep your "me" time while in a relationship that are worth a read so you can keep all the best parts of how you used your time pre-relationship. There's nothing worse than being in love with someone but not being happy because you're not taking care of yourself anymore. Remember: you are in control of your time, no matter what.

There are a lot of pearls of wisdom in this book that don't just apply to being single. Consider the bulk of Part III and all the activity and travel ideas or the much-anticipated Extras section that is full of activity and travel advice (that would have made the chapters simply painful to read through). The chapters on energy, burnout, and how you use your time are also more important than ever if you're back in a relationship where your energy is going to someone else more consistently than it ever did when you were single. Understanding how to take care of yourself so you can safely expend your mental and emotional energy to help others is an important skill to have no matter your relationship status or your stage in life. Even if your journey as a single person ends shortly after you put this book down and we part ways, keep this advice in mind to ensure your future success and happiness in all your endeavors.

The (many, many) mentions of finding and maintaining your friend group are also going to be of paramount importance when you get back into a relationship or if you're choosing to settle into singles' life. Remember: "alone" doesn't have to mean "lonely." And if you're in a relationship, remember that other types of relationships need your time and attention, too. If you're in a healthy romantic relationship, you and your partner will both have friend groups to enjoy separately. Value that time investment so that you have experiences to share when you come back together. If you're flying solo long term, then you already know how important having some social interaction is to your ability to thrive. It's probably been a little over-discussed at this point, but it's something to refer back to every now and again as you check in with yourself to make sure you're living the best life you can be.

As much fun as it is to look forward to whatever the future holds for you, in this moment, as you're reading this, you're single. A lot of advice was thrown at you and there was a lot of heavy content discussed here. Keep coming back to the relevant chapters as you hit those phases in your journey or are starting to doubt if you truly are as happy and comfortable as a single person as you could be.

This is the end of our road together for now. Hopefully you've found at least a few things you can do to improve your lifestyle and mental health and you close this book feeling understood, calm, comfortable, and happy as a single person. You've got this! (And this book is always here for when you want a reminder.) Wherever your journey leads you, always remember that you own your time and your happiness and you can become comfortable and happy however your life looks. And if you're ever feeling a little unsure about your life as a single person, this book is always here for you. Good luck on your journey!

Extras

Welcome to that often-referenced Extras section! Here you'll find lists of ideas of what to do in your free time, travel tips, journaling guides, and more! Hopefully something in here helps you gain confidence in doing something you've never done before. Enjoy!

Hobby and Activity Ideas for the Active Person (That You Can Do Without Making It Weird)

If you're the type of person who really hates just sitting around, or you have to make yourself push through sedentary activities, you'll probably find something in this list that appeals to you:

- Go for a walk
- Take a long hike
- Go for a run
- Garden
- Landscape
- Organize something
- Clean or deep clean a room
- Go shopping
- Create social media content
- Go sightseeing somewhere new and interesting
- Visit a library or museum
- Take an exercise class
- Cook something
- Try photography
- Go to an Escape Room
- Take up a sport or pick up an old high school favorite. (This is also a really fun one with friends and family. If you're from a large enough family or have enough friends, you could even be your own team!)
- Go swimming (weather permitting)
- Try water sports – Kayaking and paddle boarding are lots of fun alone or with friends

- Yoga – It's hard when you're a beginner, but it's not a super high-intensity activity, and you might be surprised by the health benefits.

There are many options for active people that depend on the weather being nice, so it's helpful to have a few indoor activities that you enjoy to mix in with any outdoor hobbies that appeal to you. And just because you see yourself as an active person doesn't mean you should skip this next section either. You might find some more sedentary activities that sound like a lot of fun, too.

Hobby and Activity Ideas for the Sedentary Person (That Won't Make You Feel Lonely)

If your idea of a perfect, relaxing day is just chilling at home, and you're not the type to go out and do something physical, there's bound to be something in this list that appeals to you. Hopefully you still read through the last list for the active options just to see if there are any ideas there. If not, head back up there and take a look. You might find something to broaden your horizon. This list isn't going anywhere!

- Sewing
- Painting
- Writing
- Reading
- Create social media content (It's interesting that this is on both lists, right? It' no surprise social media content creation can take many different forms and is both active and sedentary depending on what content you're creating. This is also something really fun to do with friends.)
- Watching new TV shows or movies (yes, this does absolutely count as a hobby!)
- Playing video games
- Physically going to the movies
- Taking a class in something sedentary
- Ceramics
- Knitting
- Rock tumbling
- Scrapbooking

- Learn a new language or brush up on an old one

If you're looking for new hobby and activity ideas, try one of these out or add them to your running list. Or try picking up a hobby you used to love when you were younger. Some of these activities may seem a little old-fashioned, but consider them nostalgic. Besides, it might be fun to take up a dying art. If there's something you're curious about, try checking your local library or bookstore for a book on the topic if you'd rather teach yourself, or check your local community center for classes or groups where you could learn. If there isn't an in-person class near you, Skillshare and other online platforms also offer tutorials on a wide variety of subjects.

Resources for Classes and Learning about Activities in Your City

We mentioned classes a few times throughout the chapters as a way to meet friends and broaden your horizons. So, how do you find classes and activities near you? There are plenty of websites you can take a look at and search by location (which also works great when you're planning a trip):
- o Trip Advisor
    - There's nothing wrong with looking at your city like you're a tourist. Trip Advisor will have recommendations for any time of year in any city. Typically, there are pages on Trip Advisor for any number of activities, experiences, and classes in a city along with location information, prices, and Trip Advisor ratings and reviews. It's a nice one-stop shop to get some names to research. There are also sometimes direct links to the business's web presence or social media where you can purchase any admission you may need or get additional details.
- o AirBnB Experiences
    - AirBnB is a fantastic site to support local businesses and individuals offering unique experiences both local to you and anywhere in the world. If you're interested in something out of the box and different, try checking out the Experiences tab on the AirBnB site. You don't always know what you're going to get

when you sign on to look at the listings, but that can be half the fun! The experiences offered might change seasonally or with anything that's going on in the city.
- o Groupon
    - Groupon is a great way to save money on packages. Businesses will offer reduced rates for some classes, activities as promotion. Be careful to read the fine print on any listing to make sure you know what you're buying. Nine times out of ten, Groupon has phenomenal deals and the businesses are thrilled to have new patrons, but there is the odd time where things don't go as planned. The good news is that Groupon has a great policy to help protect you.
- o Google
    - We all know and love Google. Google Maps is a great way to see what's in your immediate vicinity and you can always search for something specific if you want. If you're less driven by location, take a look at the Google search results for whatever class you're interested in and your area of choice. Of course, always read reviews on the places to make sure you're getting what you want, but Google has literally everything you could possibly imagine.

Staycation Ideas and Inspiration Sources

What are your options if you don't feel like traveling or you only have the night/weekend to yourself? The staycation is a perfect option for mixing things up a little without breaking the bank or taking time off of work. Staycations can be as involved and expensive as you'd like them to be, and there are fun ideas all over the Internet for staycations of all interests. A few common staycation ideas are:

- Spa kits – Spa night isn't just for women, and it doesn't have to break the bank! There are affordable spa nights for everyone if you're creative! Of course, you can always hit up a spa in your area if that's your thing. But if it's not, you can hit up a local drugstore or online store and put together a custom spa night kit for your next evening of relaxation. Some things that might be fun to include:
    - A facemask
    - A bath bomb or shower fizz tablet
    - A manicure and pedicure set
    - Aromatherapy items of your choice (lotions, diffusers, candles, etc.)
    - A nice bathrobe if you don't have one already
    - Champagne or a special drink of your choice
    - A fun snack that would typically be served at a spa

    The options are endless when it comes to ways you can pamper yourself for an evening and, of course, you're able to tailor the time and money spent to your own lifestyle. All that really matters is that you come back from your staycation feeling rested, relaxed, and pampered. There are devices and machines you can also purchase if you think you'll be doing regular spa nights such as massage pillows or mats, foot massagers, footbaths, and a wide range of other things, but those might be best left to when you're going to commit to regular spa nights (and why shouldn't you?).

- Movie night baskets – Movie nights are fun with friends and can be fun alone, too. That way you can rewind the movie as often as you want to and no one has to argue over volume control! When putting together your movie night basket, consider how many people will be there, what the movie(s) will be, and what kind of snacks and drinks you'd like to enjoy with your film. If the movie has a specific theme that can relate to food or drink, it might be fun to theme your snacks and beverages to go along with the movie. Otherwise, go nuts on all the snacks you wish you could bring into the movie theater but don't want to pay theater prices for. Some ideas are:
    - Popcorn (of course!) – there are a wide range of inexpensive popcorn flavoring mixes out there if you're not into standard microwave popcorn.
    - Theater box candy – most grocery stores carry the theater box candy in the candy aisle, and just having that special packaging will help you really feel like you're at a movie theater.

- - Soft pretzels, nachos, and hot dogs – all typical fare at American movie theaters, and you can acquire all these things or their ingredients at any grocery store for not a lot of money. It'll definitely be cheaper to make any movie theater food at home than it would be to purchase it at the theater!
  - Sodas and (in some cases) alcohol are an easy way to round out your movie snack arsenal.
  - If you want to go outside what a movie theater would serve, consider the movie you're watching and get food and drinks that go well with the theme of the movie to make it a theme night. It's a fun little extra mile that's especially appreciated with friends, but it's definitely not necessary to have a successful movie night.
- Hometown tourist – Being a tourist in your own town may sound a little odd, but it's a great way to get out for a few hours and experience your city in a new way without any major travel. Consult any of the travel resources in the section above to find some new experiences and activities in your own city that you maybe didn't know about, or go do something that you've always heard about and never got to do (or you just want to do again).
- Boardgame night (with friends) – We all know this one! And if your friends happen to be long-distance, there are plenty of apps and websites that allow you to play games virtually with a group of people so the party never has to stop!
- Backyard camping – This one may not be for everyone. It seems that people either hate or love

camping, so if you don't love camping, this might just be stressful for you. But if you have a backyard and like camping, try pitching a tent when the weather's nice and cooking food outside like you're really out camping. The upside is that if you've forgotten something, everything you could ever want is right inside, and the bathrooms will be a lot nicer! Spending time in nature and sleeping in a different environment can help you relax and recreate yourself before you start your week.

- Craft night – Now's the time to pick up that craft project you set down months ago and haven't been able to make the time to finish yet. You can also learn something new from a YouTube video or by trial and error. If you're someone who enjoys working with their hands and being creative, this might be a great way to spend an evening.
- Location-themed nights – Pick a location you've either been to and loved or haven't been to yet and pick up food from that area, watch a movie that takes place there, or listen to music from that region/town. This doesn't have to be just for international locations either. For instance, if you live in the United States and you've always wanted to visit Philadelphia, you could find a local place that serves cheesesteaks (a popular food in Philadelphia) and watch a movie or TV show set in Philadelphia such as *Rocky* or *It's Always Sunny in Philadelphia*. It's not the same as being there, but it's a fun way to change up dinner and a movie and improve your knowledge of a different city. It doesn't have to be perfect; it's just about having a good time and doing something different.

Those are just a few of the great ideas out there for a staycation. The important thing about staycations is that you're intentional about your time, and that the time you set aside for your staycation is not going to be touched by the things you'd usually do at home so you feel rested and like you had a break from your daily life. You can always mix and match any of these ideas, go and find more of your own, and include as many people you'd like to! Just have fun!

Safety Tips for Traveling Alone

If you do decide to hit the road alone, there are some things to consider about traveling safely. Being alone in a new environment can be challenging, but we've all done it, and we'll do it again at some point in our lives. So, what can we do to increase our safety and ensure better peace of mind so we can just enjoy ourselves on vacation?

- Consider taking a self-defense class before you go. Yes, this might sound a little extreme, but learning self-defense is one of the best things you can do to improve your peace of mind when traveling alone:
- Tell someone where you're staying and what your trip itinerary is.
    - This might seem like it's a little counterproductive if you're looking to get away from the typical constrains of life, but it's nice to know someone has your back so that if anything happens, someone knew when you were supposed to be home. And it's not like you have to plan your trip out to the second and provide a hyper-detailed itinerary. Just key details like the hotel you're staying at and your flight information can really help if you have a friend or family member you trust.
- Book a nicer hotel.
    - Budget motels are great for the wallet, but staying somewhere with good security and a great reputation (national chain hotels, for instance) are likely safer than roadside motels.

- Also consider if the hotel room entrance is in an interior hallway or if it has outside access. Having interior access is much safer, believe it or not.
- Don't tell anyone you're traveling alone.
- Pack pepper spray if you're able to (airlines won't allow it in carry-on bags, but you can put it in your checked luggage).
- Know your area.
  - Do some homework on where you are and where you're going so you don't look clueless when you're out and about. Doing a little homework doesn't have to take a lot of time and it will help you enjoy your trip more if you can save yourself the moments of confusion even when you're with a group.
- Try not to go out after dark (or be smart when you do).
  - We all know what can happen after dark. It's really just better to avoid it if you can, but if you're traveling in the winter or want to be out after it gets dark, just make sure you don't walk farther than you have to away from more populated areas. You can still have a good time at night!
- Check in on social media.
  - Come on—we all know it's inevitable anyway! It's fun to share your experiences on social media!
- If you drink, don't get *drunk*.
  - Getting drunk is fun for some folks, but it's always safer when you're surrounded by friends to help you get back to your room

okay. If you're traveling alone, that's not such a good idea. Just know your limits.

Budget Friendly Travel Tips and Tricks

If you're working with a tighter budget or just want to get the most for your money, there are a lot of great places to look to save a few dollars on your next trip. In a few chapters, we talked about how traveling as a group has some financial benefits when it comes to cab fare and hotel rooms, but there are plenty of ways to save even more money even if you're traveling alone.

Vacation packages are an excellent planning aid and also might save you some money on certain parts of your trip if you purchase the correct package. Since travel agencies aren't really used anymore, the Internet has become full of dozens of package options for any destination you could think of. If you're overwhelmed by the options, start by reading reviews on the websites as a whole. Odds are, if people don't have good things to say about the website, the packages won't be the best deals. However, there are a lot of great and reputable websites out there that offer excellent deals on travel packages. Consider checking out any of the websites on this list.

- Groupon
    - Pros: You can find literally anything on this website. It's searchable by both location and activity or product. Yes, Groupon also has products! Groupon is a good place to see what's available to do in a city and see how much experiences cost. Local businesses list products at a discount for Groupon users, and

- - you can also get emails with new products and experiences based on your recent searches.
  - o Cons: Groupon is not a travel website. There are getaway packages and hotels on the website, but it's not optimized for travelers. You might not be getting the absolute best deals—it's worth doing your homework. Also, make sure you read the fine print to ensure that you understand what you're purchasing.
- Expedia
  - o Pros: Expedia is a very well-established travel website. Expedia is especially great for finding hotels that are part of chains. You can shop flights, hotels, rental cars, and vacation packages. You do have some options to customize your travel package. You can also earn points when you book through Expedia.
  - o Cons: Expedia works best with a membership. It's free, but you will get promotional emails. Also, check the fine print on the reservations to make sure you know when you'll be charged. Often the advertised rates are either for members and/or for non-cancellable prepaid reservations. Another con is that if there's an issue with your reservation, you'll have to contact Expedia rather than reaching out to the entity you're renting from directly.
- Trip Advisor
  - o Pros: Trip Advisor offers more than just transportation and lodging. You can also find restaurants and read reviews here. Trip

Advisor functions much like Expedia in many other ways.
- o Cons: Don't leave your browser open too long when you're searching, and use your browser's Incognito setting to preserve any pricing. Believe it or not, the price you're shown on most travel websites will change if your browser traffic shows you've been visiting the websites often. If you're in Incognito mode, the websites can't track if you've been to the website before, and you'll get a better price.

If you have a membership to a discount club like Costco (in the United States), there are usually vacation packages available for purchase that will be discounted for members. If you're a member of AAA or AARP in North America (or something similar anywhere else in the world), you might check into the rates and available discounts out there for members of those organizations.
- Traveling on a budget
    - o Vacation packages
    - o Vacation rentals vs. hotels
    - o Belonging to rewards programs for hotels
    - o Cheap airline tickets
        - Last minute booking
        - Saving up miles
        - Credit cards with points and rewards systems
        - Flying well-priced airlines
        - Taking flights at weird times

Ready for Anything Road Trip Packing List

It's no secret that lots of us struggle with packing. It's such a common problem that countless lifestyle media outlets have published packing guides over the years to try helping us out. Here's another one to add to the list, but this time it's one that's less destination-specific, and rather travel-specific so you have all your essentials and can still travel somewhat light (we're thinking about a weekend trip at least—you may need to change the quantities):

Clothing:
- A jacket – Even if you're going somewhere super warm and tropical, bring a jacket of some kind. Not a parka, necessarily, but something warm and not bulky that you can toss on when you're going into a cooler environment. In warm climates, that's usually restaurants or shopping centers.
- Athletic shoes – You may not think you'll need them, but you'd be surprised! They're also typically annoying to try to purchase while you're at your destination and you find you want them for a longer walking day or if your feet just hurt.
- A bathing suit – Even if you had no plans for a swim or a beach day, you'd be surprised by the number of times you'll be thankful you have a swimsuit already in your bag. Especially if your hotel has a pool or a hot tub, it's nice to have the option to enjoy the amenity.

- One nice outfit – Ladies, this could mean a cocktail dress or a nice skirt and blouse. Men, some dress pants that travel well and a wrinkle-resistant dress shirt work well. You never know when you'll want to go somewhere with a dress code.

Toiletries and other life savers:
- Wrinkle spray – If you're checking a bag or have room in your luggage for an additional aerosol can, bring wrinkle spray to shake the suitcase wrinkles from your clothing when you arrive.
- Stain remover – Tide pens and Shout wipes are life savers when you're traveling, and they don't take up much room.
- A small manicure kit – a nail file and clippers at least—no one likes a broken nail while you're trying to enjoy your vacation, and it's a pain to have to spend money on something like that at a tourist shop.
- Pack your clothing with a few dryer sheets to keep them smelling fresh.
- Bring a small first-aid kit (or at least a few band aids and some antibiotic cream).
- Bring a small pack of disinfecting wipes.
- Take an extra phone charger with you – Again, tourist shops and convenience stores charge an arm and a leg for those types of things, and they break all the time.
- Extra contacts – If you wear contact lenses, bring an extra pair. Also, bring your glasses if you have them. It's kind of hard to enjoy your vacation when you're not able to see it!
- Take an extra form of ID – If you have a photo ID for your job or school that also has your name on it, that should work. Otherwise, a passport should work as

well. It's a rare occurrence, but sometimes drivers' licenses go missing and there's nothing worse than traveling without an ID.

Journaling Prompts for at Home

Journaling is a great way to get your thoughts organized and to keep a record of your past. It's also occasionally therapeutic if you have some things to get off of your chest that you just don't want to say aloud. Lots of times people will recommend journaling but won't really give you any pointers on how to get started, and it's kind of awkward at first unless you're a writer already (and even if you are, it's still hard sometimes).

The important thing to remember is that journaling is a personal thing. No one should be seeing your journal unless you give them permission, so you can write without worry of judgement. You never have to read your past entries if you don't want to. That also means that you can write however you want to. The old-fashioned recipe of "dear diary" really doesn't work for a lot of people. Some prefer to write a record of events and less of a personal narrative. Some journals read more like a series of letters. However you feel the most comfortable and whatever is natural to you is how you should journal.

If you want to start journaling, but any blank page just feels unnatural, or you don't know where to start, try purchasing a guided journal with prompts you can answer whenever you feel like it. Those journals are everywhere these days. You can find them online, in bookstores, and you can even find some free templates on the Internet if you're not nuts about spending money on a book. You can also take a look at these prompts and see if any interest you:

- If I could only remember one thing about today, what would it be?
- When I think about my childhood, the first thing I think about is…
- What shaped me into the person I am today?
- I'm looking forward to _____ this weekend.
- My ideal day off is…
- If I had an extra $10K, what would I do with it?
- I feel like I need a change. What can I shake up a little?
- Today sucked because…
- Today was fantastic because…
- Where do I want to be in a year from now?
- Where do I want to be in five years from now?
- What does my ideal self look like? How do I achieve that?
- What does my ideal life look like? How do I get there?
- My favorite memory from early adulthood is…
- Record your favorite recipe.
- List five resolutions (resolutions don't have to be just for New Year's).
- What's your favorite quote from literature or the media? Why? What does it mean to you?
- What do you have to do this weekend?
- What are you supposed to be doing right now (that you're totally putting off because you just don't want to do it)?
- If you could only take five things with you, what would you take (basic, yes, but a great way to consider your priorities)?

- Did you ever imagine a different life for yourself? If so, what was it?
- List your favorite books and a little summary of each one (but make it as hilarious as possible).
- What do you love about your job?

Journaling can be fun if you want it to be. One of the worst things you can do is treat it like a chore. If you don't feel like journaling one day, just don't! It's not schoolwork or a work task that you have to complete or there will be consequences. Journaling is supposed to relax you, so do what makes you happy.

Journaling Prompts for Travel

Another trend that's emerged recently is the travel journal. The travel journal is a fun way to remember the trips you've been on and to observe your new surroundings through a different lens. There are a lot of travel journals you can buy at a bookstore, and they're great for allowing yourself to think outside the box. There are some with prompts already listed, some with spots for photos you've taken or ticket stubs you've saved, and there are some that are mostly blank for your imagination to run wild.

If you happen to be of the creative sort, you could also create one of your own. Just get a smaller book and start laying out how you think you'll use the travel journal (not that it can't change later—that's the fun part).

Travel journals aren't just for that big trip you take once a year; you can also fill the pages with day trips, weekends away, and any other outing you'd like to remember. Just have fun with it! Travel journals are also fun to share with others sometimes, so keep that in mind as you're recording things if you plan on showing your family or friends artifacts from your trip once you have them in your journal.

These types of journals, if you buy a guided one, often have questions or prompts you can answer while you're on the trip that will help you get the most out of your travels. When you're new to travel journaling, it might be nice to pick up an inexpensive one that contains some prompts to help guide you in fully appreciating your new environment. It's also kind of fun to take an hour and just fill it out and see what happens. Of course, you don't have to fill all the pages every trip—the journal is supposed to enrich your travels, not stress you out. So, make it whatever you want!

If you're planning on building your own travel journal or want to incorporate the travel journal idea into your regular journaling adventures, here are some ideas that are great for the traveler:

- If you're into drawing, include some sketches of your new location.
- Try a collage page of photos from your trip with notes about the location and what you did there.
- People watch and write down what you think their lives are like (for the storyteller and daydreamer).
- Save ticket stubs and receipts from memorable activities and write a little something about your experience next to them on the page.
- Write a letter to a specific place. (This may sound weird, but it's kind of fun to have a one-sided conversation with a building or location. You can let your imagination run wild.)

If you're not the type that wants to (or can) put a lot of time and effort into travel journaling and you still want to do it, consider answering some of these prompts instead:

- Why did you come here?
- What have you done today?
- What are you looking forward to?
- What's the best thing you've eaten here?
- Ask a local where to go for lunch and write a review on the spot.

- Would you want to live at your destination for any amount of time? Why or why not?
- Can you see yourself ever coming back there? Why or why not?
- What's one thing you would change about your trip?
- What have you learned on your travel?
- Are you glad you came?
- You're in a location where no one really knows you. What's one thing you've always wished you could do while anonymous? Do it (if it's safe, etc.) and write about it.
- Imagine a day in your life if you were a local.
- Make a list of things you'd like to do if you go back one day.
- What's the vibe you get from your vacation locale?

These are just a few prompts to consider as you're traveling and want to write about it. There are also printed guides you can pick up from bookstores, both online and at storefronts, that will help you experience your trip in new and different ways. It might be worth picking one up or at least leafing through it to get some ideas. If you're environmentally conscious, there are refillable travel journals that you don't have to feel bad about using and you can keep building on it as you travel. And if you want to mix things up, bring a few different pens along with you to make things fun. Of course, travel light, but it's fun to make it feel a little more special.

www.ingramcontent.com/pod-product-compliance
Lightning Source LLC
Chambersburg PA
CBHW071451070526
44578CB00001B/299